The
Essence
of
Strategic
Giving

The Essence *of* Strategic Giving

A PRACTICAL GUIDE

FOR DONORS

AND FUNDRAISERS

Peter Frumkin

The University of Chicago Press

Chicago and London

PETER FRUMKIN is professor of public affairs at the Lyndon B.
Johnson School of Public Affairs and director of the RGK Center
for Philanthropy and Community Service, both at the University of
Texas at Austin. He is the author of *On Being Nonprofit: A Conceptual
and Policy Primer*; *Strategic Giving: The Art and Science of Philanthropy*,
published by the University of Chicago Press; and coauthor of *Serving
Country and Community: Who Benefits from National Service?*

The University of Chicago Press, Chicago 60637
The University of Chicago Press, Ltd., London
© 2006, 2010 by The University of Chicago
All rights reserved. Published 2010
Printed in the United States of America

This is a condensed and revised version of *Strategic Giving: The Art
and Science of Philanthropy* by Peter Frumkin.

19 18 17 16 15 14 13 12 11 10   1 2 3 4 5

ISBN-13: 978-0-226-26627-5 (paper)
ISBN-10: 0-226-26627-3 (paper)

Library of Congress Cataloging-in-Publication Data

Frumkin, Peter.
  The essence of strategic giving: a practical guide for donors and
fundraisers / Peter Frumkin.
     p. cm.
  Includes index.
  ISBN-13: 978-0-226-26627-5 (pbk.: alk. paper)
  ISBN-10: 0-226-26627-3 (pbk.: alk. paper) 1. Charity organization.
2. Deferred giving. 3. Endowments. I. Title.
  HV41.2.F78 2010
  658.15'224—dc22   2009050081

⊖ The paper used in this publication meets the minimum
requirements of the American National Standard for Information
Sciences—Permanence of Paper for Printed Library Materials,
ANSI Z39.48-1992.

Contents

Preface

Sometimes, less is more. I sincerely hope this is the case when it comes to books about philanthropy. Ten years ago, I began the long process of trying to figure out what strategy in the world of philanthropy might look like. Over time, I met with hundreds of donors, large and small, and spoke with them about their philanthropy. As they described their experiences practicing what John D. Rockefeller once called "the difficult art of giving," I searched for a common thread to their experiences and for the recurrent characteristics of their most satisfying and successful grants. The result was *Strategic Giving: The Art and Science of Philanthropy*, which turned out to be a very long book, tackling a very "difficult" subject. Not only did it offer an original conception of philanthropic strategy, but it also made an argument about the historical evolution of philanthropic practices, as well as the role of philanthropy in a democratic society. In producing this new, condensed, and revised version of my earlier book, my aim has been to focus on the core practical lessons for donors. As private philanthropy continues to grow in scope and ambition, the number of people who will wrestle with the question of how to rigorously think about their giving will only increase in the coming years. This book is for these donors, the professionals who work with them, and for all those who want to understand the logic of philanthropy.

This book thus has a simple goal: to clearly and succinctly communicate a way of thinking about strategy in the world of philanthropy. While there are dozens of books claiming to define strategy as it pertains to business, there have been very few attempts to explain what strategy might look like in the context of philanthropy. My assumption when I initially took on the original larger project was that the nature of a sound strategy probably has different constitutive elements when the goal is not to make money, but to give it away wisely. And while some might think that making money is much harder than giving it away, those who have experience with philanthropy know better.

Strategy in philanthropy turns out to be complex precisely because there is no simple bottom line against which to measure the efficacy of decisions. Many donors struggle mightily with their giving precisely because they do not have a concrete, quantifiable bottom line against which to measure. This is due in part to the fact that much of philanthropy is directed at addressing human problems that are multifaceted, do not have single solutions, and are often shaped by a huge range of factors that lie outside the span of control of the donor or the organization delivering the actual charitable service. In this context of causal uncertainty and ambiguity, donors would appear to have their work cut out for them. However, there is more. Philanthropy is even more challenging because donors are trying to both meet critical community needs through their giving and stay true to their deepest personal beliefs and social commitments. Not surprisingly, the instrumental and expressive dimensions of giving can and often do come into tension, further complicating the search for philanthropy that is both effective and satisfying. Within this conflicted and contested terrain, I offer a modest road map.

Throughout my exposition here, I remain studiously neutral on substance, not wanting to enter into the question of what the best fields for philanthropy might be. This is because almost any field of philanthropic activity can be carried out strategically and effectively. What matters more to me than what donors choose to support is that their giving is reflective and well conceived. My universal model for strategic giving has five elements. After a short introduction to the big issue in philanthropy today, I present these elements successively in the middle chapters. The five essential challenges that donors need to confront as they begin to chart their philanthropic plans are

1. Declaring the public value to be produced through their private giving.
2. Defining the grantmaking methodology that will guide this work and the theory of change that will be pursued.
3. Finding a giving style and profile level that are satisfying and productive.
4. Settling on a time frame and a pace of fund disbursement to guide their giving.
5. Selecting the kind of institution through which they will conduct their giving.

Readers should start and end with the first and last chapters. In between, the exposition of the five elements of strategy in the middle of the book allows readers to jump around and explore as they see fit.

Within each of these five dimensions, many possible choices are possible. No single answer to any of these five conceptual challenges is inherently better than another. However, it is quite clear that some sets of answers fit better together across these five dimensions. The single most important argument made in the entire book is that strategic giving involves the achievement of fit, coherence, and alignment of the five important philanthropic dimensions. Constructing a coherent strategy in philanthropy involves working tirelessly—both initially and continuously over time—to get all five elements aligned with one another. If this challenge is met, donors will know that they are engaged in a strategic approach to giving.

In my original book, I went beyond the elements of strategic giving and examined the overarching question of what constitutes effective philanthropy. I made the argument that the most effective forms of philanthropy involve the complex interaction of the private values of donors and the problems of real significance in the world around them, and that the delicate balance of expressive and instrumental content is hard to strike. On top of this broad claim were layered many other claims about wise giving, including what I hope is a compelling critique of the move to professionalize philanthropy. There were excursions into the precise nature and definability of public needs, along with a detailed treatment of evaluation and impact assessment. Much of this material is abridged in this revised version so that the focus can fall squarely on the elements of a strategic approach to giving.

In the quest for brevity and readability, the original notes and bibliography have also been sacrificed. In this shorter version, I have thus stripped away the scholarly apparatus that enveloped the larger book. However, for readers interested in exploring in greater depth many of the topics taken up here, the bibliography in *Strategic Giving* may be a useful starting point. It will point the reader to hundreds of additional ideas and source materials related to philanthropy.

Since the publication of *Strategic Giving*, I have had the pleasure of presenting my ideas to many different groups around the country and abroad, including associations of grantmakers, of clients of investment banks, and, not surprisingly, of fundraisers who want to understand the objectives and ambitions of major donors. I have learned a great deal from these interactions, and this book reflects the comments and insights of leaders from the world of practice who live and breathe these challenges daily.

I remain obligated to all the people who helped me over the years to develop and formulate the original argument about strategic giving. More recently, I have picked up a special new obligation to Anastasia Kolendo, who worked with me to abridge my original book from its former full-bodied shape to its new slender profile. I am also grateful to the talented and dedicated faculty and staff at the RGK Center for Philanthropy and Community Service at the University of Texas at Austin, where this small book took shape in a supportive environment, and to the many donors to the RGK Center who have invested in ideas and believed in their power to shape and improve practice.

CHAPTER ONE

The Idea of Strategic Giving

Two words—charity and philanthropy—are often used to describe the act of giving. Each has a special meaning that is grounded in the evolution of giving in the United States. While some have tried to simplify the connection between these two words by positing them to be incompatible or by imposing a historical or developmental order to them, the reality is that both charity and philanthropy have long operated in parallel.

Charity can best be understood as the uncomplicated and unconditional transfer of money or other assistance to those in need with the intent of helping. Though charity includes gifts of time, here I will focus on gifts of money. Charity has a long history, one that is deeply intertwined with many of the world's religions. Within Christianity, faith and charity have long gone hand in hand. In other faiths, charity has also been a central principle, a way of demonstrating caring and commitment. Charity is based on the presumption that no human being should live in misery and suffering, and that those with the ability have an obligation to help.

In modern times, charity has certainly had its critics. One argument against charity warns that by offering a handout rather than a hand up, charity reinforces social hierarchy as well as debases and humiliates the poor by forcing them to receive funds they have not earned. Second, critics say charity focuses only on the temporary alleviation of social problems like poverty. A third worry is that charity lacks professionalism. Even after decades of growth of social work as a profession, critics still worry about the training and capacity of charity workers to fashion informed and sophisticated responses to human suffering. Fourth, critics charge that charities create expectations of further private action, which makes the case for government action less compelling and broad systematic interventions difficult. Still, the urge to help those in desperate straits is strong, and the fact that this help may not get to the root of all social problems hardly means that aid should not be rendered to those in need.

What could be done to remedy some of these real and perceived flaws of charity? A new vision of helping and giving was conjured, one in which charity would be transformed into philanthropy. At the very center of the philanthropic alternative to charity are the principles of self-help and opportunity creation. In fact, these two principles were originally thought to differentiate philanthropy from old-fashioned charity so significantly that many still believe the elaboration of this distinction was *the* critical historical juncture in the evolution of giving.

Rather than just give the poor small alms on an ongoing basis, philanthropy aspires to do something more lasting and radical. By providing help to those willing to help themselves, many of the early donors believed they were improving on the model of charity by getting to the root causes of poverty and despair. Benjamin Franklin was a great proponent of philanthropy and argued against perpetual charity. His most famous dictum was that a razor could be given to those in need as a tool for self-care, one that would teach them the joys of self-help, free them from the dull and rusted razors of barbers, and give them a sense of satisfaction stemming from the money they saved. Andrew Carnegie felt that a modest lifestyle and philanthropy were duties of the rich. He also believed that philanthropy should never degenerate into mere almsgiving. Instead, serious giving should stimulate people to help themselves. Carnegie summed up his ethos of self-help: "The best means of benefiting the community is to place within its reach the ladders upon which the aspiring can rise." Since then, donors have continued to expand on this idea of intervention. With some simplification, it is possible to isolate at least five important purposes or functions that have emerged over time as philanthropy has sought to define a distinctive place for itself in public life.

One of the most common arguments about the function of philanthropy focuses on the ability of donors to use private funds to create social and political change. The use of private funds allows philanthropy to pursue a change agenda without having to spend large amounts of time mobilizing other sources of support, but also without achieving consensus among those affected. Of course, this power to deploy money in the name of political and social change makes many worry about the accountability of philanthropy.

A second function of philanthropy is to locate and support important social innovations, whether in the forms of research or programmatic breakthroughs. The freedom of choice and the absence of strong accountability mechanisms enable donors to strike out in new and unpredictable directions. Many donors give with the goal of generating new ways to conceptualize and respond to problems, though sometimes the effectiveness of social innovations is contested. Still, by enabling social entrepreneurship, philanthropy has the capacity for profound impact.

A third purpose of philanthropy—to achieve a small measure of equity through the simple redistribution of resources—is pursued by a large number of donors, particularly smaller contributors. Equity or redistributive giving is most often embedded in programs and services designed to provide long-term solutions to the problems facing the needy and often takes a local form, where caring is expressed for those in the community who are less well-off and where the concept of equity is more manageable. The equity-seeking, redistributive function of charitable giving is thus the least controversial of philanthropy functions.

A fourth rationale for philanthropy is the pure and unapologetic affirmation of pluralism as a civic value. The fact that hundreds of billions of dollars are applied each year to public purposes by disparate groups of individuals and private institutions, rather than by government, holds forth the possibility that pluralism as a value is affirmed. Giving allows a multiplicity of ideas and programs to exist in the public domain, rather than a limited number of "preferred" solutions. The argument that philanthropy affirms pluralism strikes some as both inefficient and undemocratic, in that private parties are acting in competing fashions rather than through a single, democratically selected course of action. Given the overlay of private interests on public needs that occurs when gifts are made, these shortcomings may not be a problem. After all, with a myriad of competing conceptions of the public good, power within philanthropy is dispersed and stable.

Philanthropy's fifth core function is to support the self-actualization of donors by helping givers translate their values into action. To date, this critical fifth function of philanthropy has largely been ignored, or treated with suspicion and contempt when acknowledged. After all, some might ask why one should care about the psychic benefits generated by giving when the needs of communities are so desperate. The answer lies in the complex dependence of philanthropy on the goodwill and motivation of donors. Without validating and taking seriously the donor side of philanthropy, the field runs a risk of failing to provide a viable long-term explanation for philanthropy's continued growth and its ability to carry out any of its other more public purposes. Make no mistake: Philanthropy can and should be about producing public benefits. However, it can and should also be about presenting the giver the chance to enjoy the fruits of philanthropy in the form of psychic satisfaction. In many cases, philanthropy performs an essential service of allowing individuals to find meaning and purpose in their lives. In the best cases, the interaction of the public and expressive dimensions leads toward mutual reinforcement. On this account, philanthropy is simultaneously about enacting and expressing the values of the donor and achieving public purposes.

In the end, the meaning of philanthropy is negotiated and defined every time donors and recipients are joined together through philanthropy. Philanthropy translates the private expressive desires of donors into public action aimed at meeting public needs. It has both public and private functions, enabling communities to solve problems and allowing individuals to express and enact their values. What makes philanthropy at once exciting and perplexing is the strange and at times jarring interaction of public needs and private choices that giving promotes. While philanthropy may begin with the individual's impulse to help others, it often ends in a set of relations and arrangements that may or may not achieve this simple end.

Effectiveness, Accountability, and Legitimacy

Philanthropy is a field in which donors give freely to others, and it is hard to imagine why any problems at all would be associated with the simple exercise of generosity. The philanthropic exchange linking donor and recipient can take innumerable forms, but the basic structure of the relationship remains fairly straightforward. Donors and recipients are joined in an act of giving and getting. Even though this voluntary transfer of resources seems simple, it can and does create a number of complex challenges for both sides, particularly when the amounts of money changing hands are significant and when the public needs to be addressed are substantial. Today there can be little doubt that important problems lurk within both individual and institutional giving, and that leaders within the field have expended large amounts of effort and resources searching for solutions. At the core of the angst within philanthropy are three complex and intertwined issues that have long confronted donors of all kinds: effectiveness, accountability, and legitimacy.

It is hard to imagine donors faced with the choice of "being effective" or "being ineffective" in their giving who would consciously opt for ineffectiveness. People engage in giving because they want to accomplish something, either for someone else or for themselves, or for both. In all three cases, if being effective means achieving one's stated objectives, effectiveness is as close to a universal aspiration in the balkanized field of philanthropy as one is likely to encounter. The problem is that this consensus is thin and has little practical meaning. Donors do not agree on how to define philanthropic objectives, how to assess whether they have been realized, and, perhaps most importantly of all, how to use knowledge and experience to improve their work over time.

The most popular model of assessing effectiveness today is program effectiveness, which looks at the impact of the work done by those who receive philanthropic support. With program effectiveness, protocols, procedures, and tools that can be used to carry out assessments are well established. Data showing which organizations are more effective compared to their peers can be used to deploy philanthropic resources more effectively and guard against criticism that philanthropic decisions are based on something other than merit. Unfortunately, the performance data used in the nonprofit sector is often incomplete, unreliable, and incommensurable. Measures of program effectiveness are almost never taken using formal experimental techniques (control and treatment groups) and almost always have a number of assumptions embedded within them. Regardless of these technical limitations, the concept of program effectiveness is widely used today. Complicating the measurement problems related to program effectiveness is the issue of the relative size, timing, and conditions under which a philanthropic contribution is delivered. Consider the following two grants: the first small and given late in the fund-raising process, the second large, coming at a critical early stage, and accompanied by technical assistance. Clearly, both donors should not be considered equally effective based solely on the recipient's eventual success. The issue of program effectiveness in philanthropy cannot be separated from the donor's relative philanthropic contribution. Effectiveness—even the narrow concept of program effectiveness—requires a meaningful causal link between the giving and the results. The more donors do to make gifts meaningful, the more supportable their claims of effectiveness become.

An alternative conception of effectiveness—"mission effectiveness"—looks at the quality of the grantmaking and donors' success at achieving their stated goals. It is a measure of overall impact that is far broader than whether a grantee executes well on a particular funded program. It turns the effectiveness question toward the donor and away from the grantee. When in addition to meeting specific public needs donors have other goals, like self-actualization or creation of knowledge, these objectives also become part of assessing mission effectiveness. Mission effectiveness is not simply the sum of the programmatic effects achieved by nonprofits, but is instead related to the quality of strategy and level of execution achieved by the donor. To be mission effective is to achieve one's philanthropic objectives. It is even more elusive than the concept of program effectiveness.

ACCOUNTABILITY

Even if a donor scales the effectiveness wall, there is another substantial obstacle just ahead: the problem of accountability. One of the nagging issues in philanthropy today is whether donors are ever held adequately accountable for their giving. The accountability issue arises in part from the tax deduction that donors receive for their giving, but it is also connected to the power that donors have in philanthropy to use resources to enact agendas. Interestingly, the accountability issue is more pressing in some parts of the field than in others. For individual donors who operate quietly or who give only modest amounts of money, there are rarely groups complaining about access, transparency, and fairness. For large institutional donors, including private, corporate, and community foundations, the accountability issue is far more pressing. These donors face several organized and mobilized watchdog groups that do nothing but monitor and critique foundation practices. At the center of the accountability issue is the concern that philanthropy's fundamental power asymmetry between donor and recipient makes it very hard to create accountability systems appropriate for a field that now delivers hundreds of billions of dollars a year.

The most significant step taken to address accountability concerns has been the movement to offer increased procedural accountability or transparency, particularly within the world of private foundations. The most common transparency move involves the simple release of information. Institutional donors have set up elaborate and informative web pages, published annual reports in ever greater numbers, issued concise grantmaking guidelines explaining what the donor intends to fund, and released concept papers laying out assumptions and preferred approaches to particular problems. This transparency work has produced greater understanding of the field of philanthropy among the general public and allowed nonprofit organizations to research and direct their funding proposals more efficiently.

Yet moving information about process into the open is neither the functional nor moral equivalent to creating an accountability mechanism anchored in substance. Instead of a dialogue between the world of philanthropy and its many stakeholders, transparency is pursued by donors as a long and uninterrupted monologue, offering the world information and making no real commitment to listen or to respond to feedback. To be sure, a few large foundations have experimented with surveys of their grant recipients. Even with a promise of anonymity to respondents, however, it has been a struggle to elicit honest comments. Moreover, these surveys may provide some insight into how nonprofits are treated by foundation staff, but they provide no information on the substantive issue of whether wise philanthropic choices and effective grants are being made. What is needed is substantive—not process—accountability, grounded in real efforts to measure whether the donor's goals are being achieved.

When accountability systems focus on the transparency and efficiency of grantmaking processes rather than effectiveness, donors neither advance their field by creating usable knowledge and program models, nor meet their ethical obligation to be accountable to their communities. Releasing information about how to apply for a grant and which organizations received grants in the past may make the process appear less mysterious, but these actions are still a weak proxy for real accountability systems linked to evidence of effectiveness.

LEGITIMACY

Lurking above effectiveness and accountability is the even bigger question of philanthropic legitimacy, an issue that rarely gets explored and debated. Legitimacy is a touchy issue in philanthropy. Fueled by private wealth but directed at producing public benefits, philanthropy has a built-in tension. On the one hand, it is tempting to ask who has the right to say anything about how individuals and institutions carry out their philanthropic work. These are private funds that supplement public programs, and they should simply be welcomed as a voluntary contribution to the improvement of society. On the other hand, one wonders who exactly these wealthy actors are to take it unto themselves to interpret public needs and to act as miniature and undemocratic regimes. There is a part of philanthropy, the speaking for others without their consent or consultation, that seems to require a fair amount of hubris and that is off-putting to some. Given this tension, one can reasonably ask when and why the exercise of philanthropic power is just and rightful. It is this line of thought that leads directly to the question of what makes philanthropy legitimate. The answer to the legitimacy challenge is actually painfully clear. It is impossible to be legitimate without being substantively accountable. It is impossible to be substantively accountable without credible measures of effectiveness.

Naturally, the issues of effectiveness, accountability, and legitimacy intersect and interact with one another frequently. In the absence of good measurement of goal achievement and effectiveness, many donors turn to measures of the quality of their grantmaking process and emphasize their transparency, clarity of purpose, and accountability. Similarly, when charges are leveled that donors have not acted responsibly in the way they have disbursed funds, the indictment often comes in the form of complaints about missed opportunities, lack of impact, and generally ineffective grantmaking. Effectiveness, accountability, and legitimacy are thus linked together at a deep level.

My argument ahead is that constructing and acting upon a sound philanthropic strategy is a critical way for both individual and institutional donors to answer lingering questions about philanthropy's effectiveness, its accountability, and, most significantly, its legitimacy. While strategy has long been neglected in philanthropy (at least in comparison to the business world, where strategy models abound), it is a linchpin concept. In many ways, strategic giving is the start of the yellow brick road that leads directly to effectiveness, which then opens the way to accountability and legitimacy. The model of strategic giving presented in the rest of this book is designed to provide a road map to donors who want to answer the challenges that face the field by grounding their giving in a more strategic approach. What follows is an attempt to sketch a theory of effective philanthropy that is built around a simple strategy model. To introduce the model, it may be helpful to look at two contemporary donors, their struggles and their triumphs. From there, we can begin to build a detailed framework for strategic giving.

A Tale of Two Donors

We begin with Henry and Edith Everett, wealthy New Yorkers who both enjoyed considerable professional success during their careers with investment firms. In the 1950s, they created a small family foundation, the Everett Foundation, which would serve as their vehicle for philanthropy over the coming decades. By the mid-1990s, the foundation had assets of over $10 million, which allowed the Everetts to be modest but serious donors by New York City's lofty standards. Living on the Upper East Side, the Everetts were neighbors of New York's Central Park Zoo, an institution with a long and successful history of educating adults and children about wildlife. The Central Park Zoo and the city's four other zoos were all operated by the nonprofit Wildlife Conservation Society (WCS).

One long-standing tradition at the zoo was its famous Children's Zoo, which featured a motley group of farm animals that children could visit and pet in a setting focused on children's fairy tales, including a large Mother Hubbard's shoe filled with animals, cottages for the Three Little Pigs, and a gingerbread house. The Children's Zoo, however, had fallen into disrepair. A major conflict also raged over whether the zoo should restore the fanciful 1960s exhibits or create a more naturalistic environment. After legal wrangling with architectural historians, the zoo moved forward with a compromise plan that would preserve the interactive petting zoo idea while creating a more natural environment. In early 1996, the zoo began to search for donors to support this major capital project.

After reading about the Children's Zoo's struggles in the *New York Times* and listening to friends with young children and grandchildren bemoan the extended period the institution had been closed, the Everetts decided to approach the Wildlife Conservation Society and offer their support for the renovation of the Children's Zoo. The Everetts' interest in helping coincided with WCS's need to expand its base of support. WCS had a tradition of working quietly with major donors, many of whom were board members. When needs arose, supporters such as Brooke Astor, Laurance S. Rockefeller, and Lila Acheson Wallace would gracefully reach for their checkbooks so that the organization's work could move forward. After dipping deeply into its pool of longtime supporters to meet its ambitious fundraising objectives in the 1980s, WCS sought to find new supporters who might be drawn to a wildlife preservation and education mission. The society realized that these new donors might seek more recognition than old-line donors, and that naming opportunities—naming a building, plaza, or edifice after a donor—might be a key tool for attracting contributors who had earned their fortunes in the technology and finance fields.

The Everetts were the model of the new donors that WCS was eyeing. They had been major contributors to Democratic political candidates and important Jewish philanthropic initiatives in the United States and abroad. They had made gifts to the Dance Theatre of Harlem's Everett Center for the Performing Arts, a lecture series at the New York Public Library, and an Everett Children's Adventure Garden at the New York Botanical Garden, as well as supporting anti-tobacco campaigns aimed at keeping children from starting to smoke. While the Everetts avoided the New York social scene, they were active volunteers for many years, served on numerous boards, and devoted the majority of their time to nonprofit, civic, and cultural causes. The Children's Zoo seemed like a natural fit, and the Everetts wasted no time in setting up a meeting with the president of WCS.

At this first meeting, the Everetts surprised zoo officials with a generous offer of $3 million for the estimated restoration budget of $5.9 million. It was agreed that the completed facility would be known as the Everett Children's Zoo, though exact details would need to be worked out in consultation with the zoo's many constituents and stakeholders. After working on the design and securing support for the renovation plan from all parties except the Landmark Preservation and Art commissions, WCS and the Everetts signed a contract and a first installment of $750,000 was paid. As with all their gifts, the Everetts sought and secured wording in the agreement requiring that WCS bar tobacco companies from sponsoring any event or having any association with the Everett Children's Zoo.

Henry Everett, who thought of himself as a hands-on donor, lost no time in working with WCS on the project. Visiting other children's zoos when he traveled, Everett sent in design ideas and suggestions to WCS executives. Soon, however, the relationship began to fray. Delays in getting final approval, a failure to publicly announce the gift, and disagreements about the final design exposed differences between the WCS board and the Everetts. One particularly sensitive issue was how the Everetts' name would be displayed on the zoo's entrance. Something was needed that would satisfy the Everetts while acknowledging the initial donors. The Children's Zoo entrance featured three large granite columns supporting a bronze arch with figures of animals. On the center column in large letters was "Children's Zoo," and beneath this was a plaque recognizing former Governor Herbert Lehman and his wife, Edith. According to WCS, the Everetts wanted their name carved in the granite above the existing words to create the effect of the "Everett Children's Zoo." This would be accompanied by a plaque underneath acknowledging their gift, which would cover the original acknowledgment of the Lehman gift. A new plaque on one of the side columns was to give credit to the Lehmans for the Children's Zoo's creation. The Art Commission reviewed this proposal and rejected it along with a plan for a plaque with four-inch letters for the Everetts. Instead, the commission proposed a smaller plaque with two-inch letters for the Everetts on the center column and smaller plaques on the other outside columns acknowledging the Lehmans—a solution that avoided any new carving of the granite.

Amidst all this negotiation and tension, the agreement between donor and recipient fell apart. According to the Everetts, WCS asked them to write a letter stating that they were withdrawing their gift because the contract had been breached, a letter that the zoo could then use with the Art Commission as leverage in resolving the logjam. The Everetts faxed the letter to the WCS for use in strategic bargaining with the Art Commission the following day. However, the Everetts learned that the letter was never shown, and the commission approved a new design for the arch that the Everetts never saw. For Henry and Edith Everett, this was the straw that broke the donor's back and they finalized their decision to withdraw their support. Public criticism and bad publicity would soon ensue, as their perceived pettiness was spread across the pages of New York's newspapers.

The final resolution of this entire philanthropic imbroglio involved an ironic twist. On May 15, the same day as the Everetts' decision to withdraw their gift was first publicized, James Tisch was elected president of the United Jewish Appeal-Federation of Jewish Philanthropies of New York City (UJA-Federation). Tisch was part of the prominent family in control of the Loews Corporation, which owned Lorillard Tobacco, the manufacturer of numerous brands of cigarettes. UJA-Federation board member Henry Everett had mounted a campaign to block Tisch's election to head the philanthropy on the grounds that no one involved in tobacco should head an organization dedicated to doing good work. His efforts failed and Tisch became chair of UJA-Federation. To make matters worse for the Everetts, five days later the press announced that new donors had come forward to replace the Everetts' gift to the zoo with an even more generous offer of $4.5 million. The donors were none other than Preston Tisch and his brother Laurence Tisch, father of James. In a letter to the WCS, Henry Everett wrote: "A Tisch Children's Zoo would not only represent a personal vendetta against us and the values we try to espouse but, more importantly, be a cynical rebuke of the children of our town." The Everetts never heard back from WCS.

Consider by way of contrast the experience of another donor. For much of her life, Irene Diamond's claim to fame stemmed from her career in the 1940s, when she worked as a producer in Hollywood and spotted a rough script called *Rick's Bar*. Though she never received much credit for her work, Irene Diamond helped guide this script through development into the blockbuster film *Casablanca*. By the time she was in her eighties, Irene Diamond's eye for good projects earned her widespread recognition in the world of philanthropy as well.

When her husband, Aaron Diamond, a New York real estate developer, died in 1984, Irene Diamond was left with the philanthropic task of giving away $200 million in ten years. While the Diamonds had created a foundation through which to conduct their philanthropy, they decided not to give away their funds in small increments in perpetuity. Instead, they agreed that the money should be given away over a decade by whoever survived the other. They would focus on three main areas: medical research, minority education, and cultural programs. One explanation for their decision not to set up a conventional foundation was that both Diamonds disliked bureaucracies and did not want their legacy to be a philanthropic institution that spent large amounts on overhead instead of grants. Also, both were impatient and preferred quick decisive action. Still, the task of giving away the funds was not easy for Irene Diamond, given the competing claims of various New York charities. To help her in the task, Diamond engaged an experienced grantmaker and consultant to donors to help her examine her options.

Knowing of her husband's interest in medical research, Irene Diamond became interested in the burgeoning AIDS crisis gripping New York City in the 1980s. A meeting between the city's health commissioner and Irene Diamond was brokered by the president of Sloan-Kettering Cancer Center in August 1988 to explore ways in which the Aaron Diamond Foundation might work with the city to address the AIDS crisis. The commissioner pressed Diamond to help create an independent AIDS research laboratory. The city would move quickly to supply a facility if Diamond would help fund the research and use her influence in New York to convince other individuals and foundations to contribute to the effort.

Diamond considered doing exactly what the city asked, namely, working to build support for the effort among a group of funders, and then decided that this would take too long. Instead, she decided to go it alone and provide $8.5 million in private funding needed to get the laboratory up and running and an additional $21 million for postdoctoral fellowships. The goal would be quite simple: to build the premier AIDS research laboratory in the world. The city would provide $3.5 million and lease to the new lab 22,000 square feet in a public health laboratory building in Manhattan at a rate of $1 a year for twenty years. Diamond sought immediate help with legal and licensing issues, began to work on architectural plans for the aging city building, and chose the head of Mount Sinai School of Medicine to head the search committee to find a director for the lab. The issue of who would run the lab was, of course, the most important decision facing Diamond. Eventually, Diamond and her advisors overrode the recommendations of the search committee, which favored seasoned and experienced researchers, and instead chose a young and promising researcher, still in his thirties, named David Ho.

Born in Taiwan, educated at Harvard, and teaching on the faculty of the UCLA School of Medicine, Ho had begun to make a name for himself as someone who did bold and ambitious research using polymerase chain reaction (PCR), a tool for locating and counting genes in human cells. Ho had also made waves by proving that HIV was present in far higher levels than was generally thought. Ho leaped at the opportunity to lead a major new lab, hire researchers from all over the country, and do research at the highest level. One of the earliest decisions he made as the head of the Aaron Diamond AIDS Research Center was to focus more on basic research on HIV rather than clinical research. Over time, Ho and his team's work would lead to a number of breakthroughs, the most famous of which was the discovery of protease inhibitors. When used in combination with standard anti-viral medications—especially during the early stages of infection—these "cocktails" showed great potential for combating the progression of HIV into AIDS. For his work on protease inhibitors, Ho was named *Time Magazine*'s Man of the Year, a level of recognition and celebrity signaling to all that Irene Diamond's investment in the lab and her selection of Ho had borne real fruit. Following Ho's amazingly quick and important success, Irene Diamond was recognized by the White House as a philanthropist who made a difference, profiled in magazines, and celebrated by other donors for her contributions to the field.

The Aaron Diamond AIDS Research Center has continued its work in AIDS research and expanded substantially with the infusion of public funds from the National Institutes of Health. The lab has influenced the way research is conducted at other labs and became the paradigmatic philanthropic intervention in medical research. What made this intervention so successful? Was it just luck? Why did Irene Diamond produce so much public value through her philanthropy while the Everetts' philanthropy led to such a calamitous and embarrassing failure?

It is important to dismiss a number of incomplete explanations for the different outcomes of the Everett and Diamond gifts. First, the significant difference between philanthropic targets—medical research and culture—does not explain the disparate nature of the results. After all, a children's zoo could turn out to be a major success and a search for a cure could lead nowhere. The choice of the mission alone did not predetermine the donors' degrees of success.

Second, Diamond's more leveraged approach could not fully explain the difference in impact. Gifts like Diamond's, targeted at supporting research, are risky but potentially very rewarding. If the investigators are successful, the creation of new knowledge can transform large areas of practice and lead to significant applications. Gifts to capital campaigns, like the Everetts', have a more modest but more likely potential for impact. While Diamond's giving appears to be higher risk and potentially more leveraged, this alone does not explain the outcomes achieved.

Third, assuming the structural perspective, we could argue that the particular philanthropic vehicle or institution used by the two donors determined the ultimate outcomes. However, on closer inspection, the structures deployed by both donors were not that different. While in both cases the donors were alive, in the Everetts' case the couple sought to work together through their evolving and growing foundation to achieve their goals. Irene Diamond was acting through a limited-term foundation named after her late husband. The Everetts did most of their work themselves, interacting directly with the recipient and communicating their concerns immediately to the leadership of the zoo. Irene Diamond's foundation had a small staff, though she made many of the most important philanthropic calls. In both cases, donors were working through foundations to achieve their objectives and neither reaped inordinate benefits from the choice of organizational vehicle for philanthropy.

Fourth, it would be easy to argue that the answer lies in a difference of style, temperament, and personal approach. After all, the low-key, behind-the-scenes approach of Irene Diamond stands in contrast to the Everetts' visible, engaged, and demanding philanthropic style. When Henry Everett became more engaged with the zoo, doing some research and looking at plans, he was fulfilling many donors' dream—managing his gift actively so as to produce the best possible outcome. Irene Diamond, by virtue of her decision to fund scientific research, was at an immediate disadvantage when it came to cultivating an engaged relationship. Much of her involvement was up front, providing funding and finding leadership for the lab. More to the point, there was a difference between the Everetts and Irene Diamond in the recognition sought in return for philanthropic support. The Everetts pursued to a greater or lesser extent—depending on which side of the dispute one listens to—name recognition and public profile. Irene Diamond, on the other hand, was known for her low-key approach that focused the spotlight on her projects, not herself. Even though significant stylistic differences emerge when these two tales are juxtaposed, the outcomes achieved cannot be explained in terms of personality and profile alone.

Finally, one might want to point to a major difference in time horizons. It would, however, be a gross simplification to focus on the temporal dimension of philanthropy and to assume that the ten-year time limit for the existence of the Aaron Diamond Foundation pushed Irene Diamond to achieve so much. The time-constrained feature of the Diamond Foundation led it to make a number of large philanthropic commitments in a relatively compressed period of time. It led to the selection of major actionable, urgent objectives. The use of a limited life foundation may have helped Irene Diamond take some chances, but it does not fully explain the divergent results achieved by these two foundations.

Each of these candidate explanations falls short of the mark. The presence of a strategy behind Irene Diamond's giving and a lack of clear strategy in the case of the Everetts explains these strikingly different stories. One way to think about strategy is to focus on the level of fit and alignment between the five critical elements in giving, each of which was nominated in isolation previously: the underlying value to be produced, the logic model applied, the style or level of engagement of the donor, the time frame for giving, and the philanthropic vehicle or structure selected. These elements, I argue, lie at the core of the idea of philanthropic strategy. Irene Diamond's commitment to AIDS, her use of a limited life foundation, her decision to spend money quickly rather than at a slow dribble, her focus on basic research, and her active role in setting a direction all contributed to a strategic synergy and fit that bore important public benefits. Strategy is not about finding the right answer to any one particular area, but about finding answers to the core philanthropic questions in a consistent and coherent way.

A Model of Philanthropic Strategy

To help explain the nature of strategic giving, I advance here a framework for both analyzing and informing philanthropic choices. Because philanthropy allows individuals to enact their private visions of the public good, developing a coherent strategy for giving is a difficult challenge. It is a process that can and does become controversial as the boundaries between the donor's interests and the needs of the community come into contact. Dissipating this tension by normalizing and converging philanthropy around a narrow set of acceptable practices would not be a promising approach. After all, if giving were reduced to a set of precise principles and precepts acceptable and applicable to all, much of philanthropy's variety and the capacity to innovate would likely be compromised. Most donors do not need or want a set of restrictive and substantive rules that attempt to tell them what they should support, how they should conduct their giving, or when they should make their philanthropic decisions. Instead, donors can most benefit from a simple, usable framework for thinking about all the complex issues that charitable giving raises, a framework that allows donors to make their own decisions with compassion and intelligence.

The framework presented here, while neutral on substantive issues, points to five essential questions that donors need to confront as they begin to chart their philanthropic plans. First, all donors must declare for themselves the value to be produced through their giving. This means arriving through careful consideration at an answer to the question: What is valuable to my community and me? Second, donors need to define the type and scope of program that will be supported. In so doing, they must answer the question: What kinds of nonprofit activity will work best? Third, donors must find a giving style and profile level that are satisfying and productive. In so doing, they should reflect on the question: What level of engagement and visibility do I want for my giving? Fourth, donors have to settle on a time frame that will guide their giving. This means thinking through how to respond to the question: When should my giving take place? Fifth, donors have to select a vehicle or structure through which they will conduct their giving. An answer must be readied to the question: What vehicle can best be used to accomplish my goals?

Taken in isolation, no one of these questions has a clear and unequivocally appropriate answer. However, sets of answers demonstrably fit more or less well together. This points to the following basic premise: Strategic giving can be defined as the clear alignment of the five important philanthropic dimensions described previously. Some donors will start with clear answers to one or more of the five questions. Others will approach this task of building strategy with a more open slate. In either case, constructing a coherent strategy in philanthropy involves checking and rechecking the alignment and fit of all elements in an effort to find a consistent, mutually supporting model for giving. When answers to all five questions are in complete alignment, the possibilities for social impact and donor

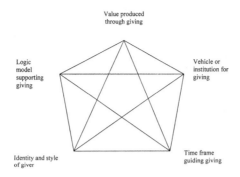

Value produced
through giving

Logic
model
supporting
giving

Vehicle or
institution for
giving

Identity and style
of giver

Time frame
guiding giving

Fig. 1.1: The philanthropic prism.

satisfaction are high. Moving toward alignment is the central task of the strategic donor.

The framework I develop (see fig. 1.1), "the philanthropic prism," can serve as a structured checklist and diagnostic device for donors. By revealing points of alignment and fit as well as points of tension and misalignment, the prism can guide donors toward philanthropic choices that are more internally consistent. Under ideal circumstances, this analytic work will be completed before donors have gone very far with their giving. However, recognizing that many people learn best by doing, the prism can also be used by those who have made many philanthropic commitments only to realize the need for greater order and discipline. Applying this strategic analysis to quagmires and contentious situations in philanthropic giving will likely isolate the trouble spots that require attention while guiding the donor toward greater levels of coherence and fit in the future.

Strategic giving must start with the definition of a core value proposition that declares a particular purpose or activity worth pursuing. This challenge can be approached from two different directions. Some donors may make a substantive commitment by turning inward, reflecting on their values and interests, and eventually seeking out organizations or causes with which they can identify. Other donors will approach this task by looking outward, researching the most pressing public needs, and locating organizations that can fulfill these needs. Of course, these two approaches are not mutually exclusive, and most donors seek to situate their giving somewhere between these two pure conceptions of giving. I suggest that the starting point should be the search for a value proposition that maximizes both the public benefits of giving and the personal satisfaction of the donor.

Donors must take steps to clarify the underlying logic model that will animate their giving. This means making a decision about a theory of change that will determine the kinds of programs funded and the expected results of these activities. Strategic giving requires contextually appropriate decisions about when to pursue "top-down" strategies aimed at changing the intellectual grounding of a field and when to seek a "bottom-up" or grassroots solution. Donors must also confront a set of more operational issues relating to the form of support supplied, be it general operating support, project grants, matching awards, loans, in-kind contributions, or capital funding. These decisions will turn on how leverage can best be gained, given the philanthropist's purpose. Finally, donors may want to think through how their giving will achieve meaningful scale, whether through organizational expansion or program replication. A logic model is important because it defines the causal linkages, starting with the making of a grant and ending with the results. Many grants do not produce each of their intended effects, and a clear logic model will give the donor the opportunity to diagnose the problem with a given philanthropic intervention. In this sense, a logic model that includes theories of change, leverage, and scale can be a potent tool for both planning and learning.

In assembling a plan for giving, donors need to think about their giving style and their philanthropic identity. In some cases, donors will seek out the advice and counsel of family members, friends, lawyers, staff, and consultants when executing their giving. A trend toward philanthropic disintermediation has, however, emerged in recent years: many wealthy entrepreneurs have decided to cut out all philanthropic assistants and middlemen, and instead look to themselves as the principal agents of their own philanthropy. Among donors, styles range from a hands-off approach, in which a check is mailed to a recipient organization, to a more deeply engaged approach, in which the donor and recipient work together on program development and problem solving. At the same time, some donors will seek to act anonymously, while others will want recognition and visibility. In deciding upon a grantmaking identity and style, donors need to do more than just assess their private comfort levels. They must ask which form of agency is most aligned with the type of program being funded and the structure through which their giving is taking place. Only when the donor's style and identity are understood in terms of their relationship with other points in the philanthropic prism is it possible to come to an assessment of effectiveness and appropriateness.

Donors are also confronted with the issue of how much to give now and how much to give later. This decision involves weighing the question of perpetuity and thinking about the appropriate payout rate for their giving. The question of when to give points to the need for a kind of "philanthropic discounting." In thinking about the payout rate for their giving, donors must assess the likely cost escalation in the field, the rate at which the problem will or will not become exacerbated over time, and the cost of deferring benefits. Donors need to make a judgment about when and at what pace their philanthropic resources should be consumed by recipient organizations, and whether the funds should be used for endowment purposes or to meet current expenses. Most importantly of all, the time frame for the donor's giving must fit the projected contour or development of the issue to be addressed. In cases in which the costs of delaying action are great—as is the case with major diseases, famines, and intense social crises—donors may need to privilege current giving. However, when the issue that the donor chooses to address is likely to be present for decades or centuries, as is the case with many global environment and population problems, a longer time frame may be needed.

Over the years, philanthropy has generated a number of distinctive organizational forms. In addition to private independent foundations (that usually exist in perpetuity and simply make grants), donors have three main institutional options: operating foundations (that use endowment interest to fund program activities carried out by foundation staff), community foundations (that solicit endowment funds from residents of the surrounding city or region), and charitable gift funds (that are operated by mutual fund companies and act as charitable checkbooks). Donors can also choose to eschew structure entirely and simply make gifts directly, or they can select a range of planned giving options. Some donors prefer to act collaboratively either through federated funders or through the growing ranks of giving circles. Donors must examine the full menu with regard to the structure of their giving and its overall fit and alignment as well as understand how philanthropic vehicles can both enable and cripple giving.

This book argues that philanthropy—particularly large-scale giving—demands some level of strategy, and that the essence of strategic philanthropy comes down to the alignment of the five points of the philanthropic prism. That is, giving only moves from being haphazard to strategic through the achievement of fit between the elements of the prism. Drawing on many cases and examples, the book concludes that the task of the strategic donor is to work on the *entirety* of the philanthropic prism until each point is defined, polished, and in alignment with the others. Only when donors have achieved this complex and challenging level of fit can they claim that their giving has truly become strategic. This leads to the final conclusion that only when giving becomes strategic will donors have a higher probability of creating value for the public and for themselves.

Are strategy and strategic alignment the be-all and end-all of philanthropy? Hardly. There will always be room and a place for disjointed, emotive, and individualistic giving that operates without a concern in the world about effectiveness and strategy, as well as for narrow and unimaginative giving that simply responds to an urgent need. Thus, my goal here is not to push donors toward an exclusive and narrow vision of strategic philanthropy as the only defensible form of giving. Instead, I want to suggest that, for those donors seeking to find both personal satisfaction from their giving and to maximize the chances of producing significant public benefits, thinking about the quality and character of one's philanthropic strategy might be useful.

This is particularly the case if philanthropic objectives are ambitious. If a donor has the modest and limited goal of recognizing and thanking the hospital that provided quality and compassionate service to the donor's family, the philanthropic task need not be excessively complicated. A simple gift will do the work at hand. If the donor wants to both recognize the fine work of the hospital and push it to continue to advance the frontier of medicine in a particular field such as orthopedic surgery, the task is suddenly more ambitious and complex. As the philanthropic intentions of donors become broader and as the clarity of their vision of the public good increases, donors begin to demand more than just personal satisfaction from their giving. They see a part of their own psychic return from engaging in philanthropy as deeply connected to the impact their giving has on society. Strategy becomes a central challenge. This model of strategic giving is directed toward donors who possess both private and public agendas.

The other factor that may be behind a demand for higher levels of strategy in giving is related to resources. With only a small amount of money to give, the donor may either eschew extensive strategic questioning or, on the contrary, feel a tremendous burden to develop and implement a strategy to maximize the impact of the funds at hand. The situation is different when resources reach hundreds of millions and now increasingly several billions of dollars. Then the call of strategic giving becomes very strong. While structuring giving in such a way as to meet the personal expressive needs of donors remains critical, it is harder for major donors to retreat from the challenge of identifying and addressing important public needs through philanthropy. Scale of resources brings with it a strategic imperative to act wisely and to give in a way that both meets the needs of the donor and those of the community.

In thinking about achieving alignment and fit among these many complex dimensions of giving, where one starts is ultimately less important than where one finishes. Many donors begin the process of strategic planning knowing what at least one of the points of the strategic prism looks like for them. They may feel committed to building a family foundation, a high level of engagement with the organizations they fund, or a short giving time frame. All other decisions then follow from these commitments. Many donors have made decisions about one or more of the five critical questions only to find that the decision must be revisited once their giving has progressed. Therefore, committing entirely to any single dimension until the broader picture emerges may be impossible. Thus, there is no profound rationale for the sequence of elements followed in this book. Building a philanthropic strategy is a circular process that involves continuous rethinking and realignment, as the donor's interests shift, as the problems demanding attention change, and as the donor's experience and expertise improve and evolve with practice.

CHAPTER TWO

Dimensions of Philanthropic Value

The choice of what to support lies at the heart of defining a strategy for giving. Donors cannot say yes to every grant-seeker who seeks support. To do so would inevitably deplete resources quickly and lead to a large disconnected group of grants. While most organizations seeking funds are deserving, basing all philanthropic decisions only on the expressed needs of organizations requesting support is impossible. Philanthropic strategy demands that donors make some effort to bring coherence and order to giving. This process starts with the definition of a mission to be pursued or a value to be produced.

In developing a philanthropic strategy, defining the value to be produced is often the starting point, but this can also be a minefield. Many donors may find it difficult to forgo options and choices in a field that is all about freedom and limitless possibilities. Moreover, many individuals begin their giving only with a vague sense of what their "philanthropic calling" might be, and they want to discover and define their mission by making grants and practicing their giving across many fields. These are good reasons for starting elsewhere in the philanthropic prism. Moreover, sometimes philanthropy must react quickly to changing circumstances and proceed from the interaction of donor commitments and events. Thus, imposing order and direction on philanthropy through value definition can be difficult.

However, even allowing for some flexibility and freedom, boundaries need to be placed on the kinds of activities that will be considered. The idea of defining a single philanthropic value may seem constraining, but should instead be understood as one in a portfolio of choices. In fact, most institutional funders choose three or four defined program areas in which to operate as a diversification strategy. For individuals, particularly newcomers, having a small number of purposes can be helpful, especially if it allows the donors to see how different fields, such as child welfare and education, have unique internal logics yet interact in complex ways. Whether through study and reflection or through experience and practice, the value commitment must be made, even if the definition of mission, purpose, or value is broad and multi-dimensional.

Public Needs and Private Values

All philanthropic activity involves a choice about how to join public needs with private commitments in a way that is both beneficial for others and satisfying for the giver. When lacking in one of these two dimensions, philanthropy can degenerate either into a bland and disconnected exercise in transfer payments or into a selfish and shallow indulgence of the leisure class. Yet the choice of what goal or mission to pursue is not a zero-sum trade-off between public benefits and private satisfaction, in which more of one implies less of the other. The most strategic forms of philanthropy are those that start with a tight and energizing link between the donor's passions and the community's needs, which leads to high levels of both public impact and private satisfaction.

Unfortunately, too many donors conceive the public and private dimensions of philanthropy as distinct and irreconcilable. From one extreme perspective, the call of philanthropy demands the conscious abrogation of the self and the pursuit of the most urgent community needs. This conception of giving is understandable, given the range of human problems like youth violence, drug abuse, failing public schools, and a lack of affordable housing that present themselves to all donors. However, this approach is rendered difficult by the lack of consensus on what constitutes a public need or even how we should approach defining one.

If the discussions in our public sphere, especially in politics, are any indication, public consensus on the prioritization or even a standard for how to define public needs does not exist. Public needs are arrived at through both collective deliberations and individual reasoning, and no simple answer exists to the question of how many people need to agree before an issue becomes a bona fide public need. Coherence and specificity may be sacrificed in the process of seeking consensus because of the inverse correlation between the number of people engaged in decision making and the ability of parties to reach a narrow and precise agreement on terms. Aside from the issue of who defines public needs, parties also differ on how these needs are defined. Positivistic definitions of public needs, which are supported empirically through field research, are posited alongside normative definitions, which frequently rely on moral arguments and are concerned with the expectations of the way things ought to be. With so many ways to define what constitutes a public need, politics has taught philanthropy that a rational hierarchy of social needs is hard to construct and defend in a way that everyone will accept.

One good indication that no clear, compelling hierarchy of charitable causes can be defined lies in the enduring reticence of the tax code to treat any particular type of nonprofit differently from all the rest. Soup kitchens receive the same tax treatments as avant-garde theaters. Community health clinics working in desperate urban settings receive no advantage compared to suburban historical societies. All public-serving nonprofit organizations are treated the same because the alternative, a differentiated treatment of charities based on their social contribution, is simply unworkable. Additionally, the actual distribution of philanthropic funds does not reveal any real discernable hierarchy of social needs. Money is distributed across many fields, with religion, higher education, and health receiving large portions of the philanthropic pie. Within these broad categories, it is very hard to ascertain what percent of donated funds are used for social justice concerns or to aid the most needy. In practice, the criteria are nebulous for defining the relative urgency of public needs.

Thus, donors find that even in seeking to identify a public need to focus on in their giving, some personal reflection is necessary. Much as in the public sphere, donors have the choice to define the public needs on their own or in collaboration with their many stakeholders. They can choose to define public needs positivistically, after reflecting on existing empirical research, or normatively, based on moral claims about what needs are important. In practice, many of the wisest donors pursue a compromise position that is a hybrid of these models, one that combines both the expressed desires of the local community and their own convictions, balancing, at the same time, the latest research and science with the most powerful and compelling moral arguments made on behalf of others.

If the nature of public needs defines one side of the conceptual playing field of philanthropy, the other side is marked by the character of the private values and commitments enacted through giving. Philanthropy allows donors to speak to the world about what they believe is valuable and can be seen as an expressive activity that allows individuals to project their values into the public space. Having earned or acquired money legitimately and under no obligation to give anything away, some wealthy individuals decide that the primary factor driving their giving should be their personal satisfaction. This may lead donors to support organizations that have been personally significant—a college that the donor attended or a hospital that prolonged the donor's life. When the private values of the donor are a starting point, the most pressing public needs may not be the only ones selected for funding. Rather, the personal life experiences and values of the donor will become a major factor.

Instead of seeking to sublimate the personal connection and passion of donors, acknowledging them and capturing their capacity to mobilize giving may be most productive. After all, on almost every major issue or topic, both sides are usually supported by their own donors. Without donors feeling some satisfaction from their giving, it is hard to imagine how the long-standing growth of giving in the United States could be sustained. Unlike taxes, which are compulsory and used without specific taxpayers' approval to cover a range of routine government expenditures, philanthropic funds can be directed to causes that matter to donors and affirm their values. This powerful point of differentiation gives philanthropy its powerful pull. For philanthropy to work, donors need to be matched to the issues that speak to them so they can see their giving as a form of expression and action on behalf of causes or missions that matter to them.

Not everyone is willing to embrace the private nature of the philanthropic impulse so quickly. Rather than accept the passions and commitments of givers as a source of strength and vitality for the field, some attempt to construe the private values as a threat to a rational and effective philanthropy. The occasionally bizarre and extreme ideas of donors must be held to some kind of account so that publicly subsidized giving can meet its full potential. Interestingly, those who have reservations about the role of private values in philanthropy tend to overlap with those who believe that philanthropy should be directed at the most pressing human needs or who want to see communities have a greater say in the allocation of philanthropic funds. Only with a nuanced point of view on the nature of public needs does the full potential value of a donor-driven, personalistic philanthropy come into full focus. Not only is it impossible to take private values out of individual philanthropy, but to do so would surely weaken the performance of philanthropy and undermine its ability to mobilize large amounts of money.

The private values of donors interact with public needs, and philanthropy is enriched when the two find some overlap. It is a complex intersection, in which private values need to find resonance with community desires. Dueling perceptions of public needs can collide and make the location of this intersection elusive. What is striking about philanthropy is that in the cases where this conflu-ence of contradictory forces has occurred, impressive results have been achieved for all parties. Nevertheless, in the many cases where this intersection is not achieved, philanthropy can and does take alternative or mixed forms that are greater or lesser approximations of strategic giving.

Four Forms of Value Creation

Although the concepts of public need and private values are highly contested and problematic, a framework for understanding the main forms of philanthropic value creation can be sketched out. To do so, giving should be understood to possess two very different di-mensions, one of which is instrumental in nature and the other of which is expressive. First, philanthropy is an important instrument for the accomplishment of public purposes, no matter how or by whom they are defined. Gifts and grants can be a central support mechanism that allows a wide range of nonprofits to offer the ser-vices on which their clients depend. When they succeed in achiev-ing public purposes, defined in any of the many possible ways, do-nors deliver something of instrumental value. As such, giving has an instrumental dimension that is measured in terms of its concrete outcomes.

Second, giving can be seen as valuable because it allows donors to express their values and commitment through gifts to others. By committing to broad causes that are close to the heart, donors can feel the powerful expressive function of giving. For donors, acting publicly can be a satisfying end unto itself, regardless of the ultimate outcome. The value created may be entirely psychic and may arise simply from the act of expressing commitment, caring, and belief. The expressive quality of giving suggests that the narrow focus on the programmatic outcomes achieved through philanthropy may dis-tract from the deeper meaning of philanthropic action, which springs from the self-actualization experienced by those who give or volun-teer. This is what I will call the expressive dimension of giving.

The expressive and instrumental dimensions of giving can complement one another, or they can create tensions. Under the right circumstances, the values that drive donors can be harnessed to produce better and more effective grantmaking. In some ways, this connection seems obvious: committed donors are more likely to work hard to create value through their giving than donors who feel detached and removed from their philanthropy. When the values, commitments, and beliefs of the donor find expression in philanthropy, they can become at odds with the instrumental purposes that the donor is seeking to achieve.

As donors deliberate over how to balance these two critical dimensions, four main options emerge. First, giving can be purged of private values and be aimed at very narrow and specific public needs: what will result, however, is a form of giving that resembles old-fashioned charity, in which money simply passes quietly and uncreatively from one person to another through an intermediary organization. Second, giving can be infused with donor values and passions and be directed at a purpose that neither the community nor the donor can reasonably argue is urgent or important. This will generate a form of expressive giving that privileges the donor's needs but that does not meet the test of effectiveness. Third, giving can be directed at the public needs of affected communities in ways that are potentially far-reaching, with the donor's values and input screened out of the equation. In such cases, a kind of instrumental giving will emerge directed at delivering results, even if innovation and passion are missing. Finally, there is a kind of giving in which public needs are successfully married with deeply held beliefs and commitments of donors. This strange and elusive combination is what I seek to illuminate here.

To better understand the interaction of these two dimensions, one can construct a map that tracks along two axes the critical difference between the instrumental and expressive dimensions of giving. The four forms of value creation presented here (see fig. 2.1) are ideal types, in that they represent pure concepts. In practice, the boundaries around these types are almost always loose and shifting.

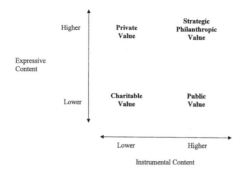

Fig. 2.1: Four forms of value creation in philanthropy.

More often than not, a donor's giving combines two or more of these types. Even with these caveats, it is still possible to begin to sketch the landscape of value creation in philanthropy by distinguishing the kinds of private commitment and public purpose that is pursued.

More Charitable Forms of Giving

In its purest form, charity starts with the recognition that not all giving is or needs to be strategic giving. A large amount of giving by individuals and even institutions is simply uncomplicated benevolence that takes the simple form of a gift. Even though I have noted earlier that charity has fallen on hard times, the concept has a long and venerable history stretching back into the earliest societies. Charity is central to almost all religious traditions and connects faith with worldly deeds. Today the perceived problem with small-scale charity is grounded in the assumption that giving needs to do more than provide assistance as crises arise in the lives of individuals and communities. As the scale of human needs on both a national and an international stage grows, there is a sense that the size of the problems are enormous compared to the capacity of small-scale, traditional charitable giving. Charity is simply too modest and local for some donors, especially those with big ambitions focusing on complex problems.

Charitable giving takes many forms. Today large amounts of charitable resources are mobilized through direct-mail fund-raising. Frequently aimed at programs serving the disadvantaged or disabled or medical research in search of a cure for a disease, these appeals ask for small contributions. The appeals are mostly aimed at getting the attention of those who receive the letters, perhaps even targeting people whose families have been touched by the disease in question and who want to do something to help others. The use of direct mail has become a very sophisticated business over the years, with appeals aimed with increasing precision at targets likely to be inclined to support a particular cause. One of the real attractions of this kind of fund-raising is that it tends to produce supporters who can be counted on in subsequent years to support a particular cause or organization. Thus, while the cost may be high in terms of finding donors within the broad universe of possible supporters, the long-term benefits of building a base of small contributors should not be underestimated. At a time when other sources of support—foundation and government grants, for example—tend to come and go over time, small donors can be counted on to supply critical unrestricted support for years at a time.

In making small contributions by mail, few if any donors ask questions about the use of their funds. Most often the funds are simply given to the charity with the expectation that the funds will be used wisely. With little investigation or follow-up from donors, the mobilization of large numbers of small contributors is attractive to organizations, providing them with unrestricted support that can be used to cover critical infrastructure expenses that institutional funders may balk at underwriting. In exchange for their donations, small direct-mail givers do receive something significant in return: a sense of having done something to help others. This is a feeling that can be bought for relatively little money and with no real commitment of time or energy. It is a form of charity that is admittedly superficial, but one that satisfies the needs of a large number of givers. It is built on a traditional model of charity, one in which the cause is preeminent and the donor is secondary. Billions of dollars are raised this way, with organizations routinely sending multimillion piece mailings across the country. Because they both tend to have a low rate of eliciting gifts and because the gifts that are produced tend to be small, direct mail seeks to compensate by increasing the volume of appeals. Direct-mail fund-raising by nonprofits has gotten very sophisticated, and it now times and directs its appeals to capitalize on such things as natural disasters, special holidays, event anniversaries, and local national policy debates in government.

One of the most ubiquitous forms of charity takes place during the holidays. Every year between Thanksgiving and Christmas, members of the Salvation Army stand on street corners shaking bells and collecting contributions from people walking by. The amount of the average contribution is small and often is simply the change bouncing about in a person's pocket as they walk down the street, but the intention of those who give is clear: to help others during the holiday season who are less fortunate. The Salvation Army is able to elicit this kind of simple and direct giving because it has a reputation for lean operations and a devotion to mission. Those who contribute small amounts to the organization do not do so with any real illusion that their individual contribution will make a major difference, but rather that the totality of small contributions may amount to something significant. In fact, the Salvation Army raises millions from its bell-ringing campaigns. Thus, when small-scale charity is channeled and organized effectively, it can reach beyond the limitations of charity and seek out larger and bolder solutions to public problems.

Although there is certainly a lasting place for charity in the broader landscape of giving, it continues to have its limitations, both as an effective instrument of change and as a vehicle for the expression of private values. When it is small and local, charity—practiced through workplace giving or in response to direct-mail and seasonal appeals—may succeed in reaching populations that others have ignored. However, the scope of the intended benefits of this kind of giving is generally limited. For this reason, donors with greater levels of resources tend to seek out opportunities that will allow them to have a broader impact and more clearly measurable effects that can be attributed to the donor's own giving. These considerations set aside, there is still no denying that on the map of value creation, a fair amount of all giving occurs with little expressive content and with very modest instrumental purposes.

More Instrumental Forms of Giving

Sometimes giving has a purposeful or instrumental rationale. Donors may give simply because they spot a problem or need for which philanthropic resources represent a solution. The substantive topic can be less important than the quality of the philanthropic opportunity and the possibility of doing good. For such donors, achieving an outcome, not enacting their private values or beliefs, is particularly attractive. The instrumental side of giving is often accentuated by the fact that many wealthy donors do not have strong passions about any particular issue and are more interested in being useful than anything else. For such donors, the instrumental side of giving looms large. It represents a relatively straightforward way to score their philanthropy, one that is not enmeshed in their personal or family lives.

In Madison, Wisconsin, a city of about 200,000, a manifestation of instrumental giving recently resulted in a massive gift to fund the creation of a major downtown arts district. Jerome Frautschi came from a family who had been in Madison for five generations and was known for the combination furniture business and funeral parlor it operated. Frautschi and his wife, Pleasant Rowland, founded their own business and quietly built the Pleasant Company, which manufactured the popular American Girl doll collection. The company was sold to Mattel in 1998 for $700 million. Because his father had always been involved in civic matters and helped raise money for the original Madison Art Center, Jerome Frautschi knew that he, too, wanted to give back something. Frautschi put aside $50 million for the arts in Madison in his newly created Overture Foundation and then raised that commitment to $100 million. The gift was equal to more than half of the city's annual tax revenue. More symbolically, the gift was larger than the entire annual grants budget of the National Endowment for the Arts. The funds were designated for the renovation of existing arts buildings and to erect new ones. To launch this complex effort, Frautschi hired the city's planning and development director to oversee what became known as the Overture Project. Eventually, the internationally known architect Cesar Pelli was hired to create the plans for the project that would meld old and new into a world-class arts complex for the residents of Madison.

Several aspects of this gift are noteworthy. First, there will be no Frautschi Arts Center, no Frautschi Hall, nor even a Frautschi rotunda in the new complex because the donor consciously chose to avoid any such arrangements. Second, the gift does not enact the values of a real arts aficionado, given that the donor's favorite forms of culture include the tunes of Andrew Lloyd Webber and adventure novels. Third and most significantly, the gift does seek to address an important civic need, one that local government has long neglected. Wisconsin ranks among the bottom states in terms of state and local support of the arts. In rationalizing his philanthropic decision, Frautschi chose to focus on something that the public sector has neglected because of its other pressing commitments. Recognizing that a division of labor between the public and private sectors was inevitable, Frautschi believed that his gift was simply taking care of something that many taxpayers would not prioritize yet that many would enjoy.

Not surprisingly, given the activist reputation of Madison, this public-spirited gift met with a fair amount of resistance. The local wish list of the arts community included exhibition spaces, dance studios, concert halls, and a theater—not all of which were being addressed by the proposed plan. Second, because the plan involved a major renovation of the existing Civic Center arts building and the construction of new buildings around it, many residents thought that the planning process needed to be more open to community input and control. A People's Arts District group was founded to attempt to slow down the fast-moving project and to ensure that what was built met the community's needs, and that not only the performing arts but also the broader cultural arts were assisted. A central point of contention was whether the Overture Project was a public project or a "civic gift." Although the funds were from a private source, the project involved the condemnation of the entire block on which the existing arts center stood so as to allow for full development. While the project continued to move forward toward completion, the boundary issue raised by even the most instrumental and public-oriented forms of philanthropy underscores the tensions that arise whenever private parties seek to act on behalf of the public.

Instrumentalism finds its most common manifestations not in the mega-gifts of individuals, but rather in the detached and often value-neutral giving practiced by major institutional donors. Many of the largest independent, corporate, and community foundations today are highly proficient when it comes to the technology of grantmaking: they efficiently process grant applications, conduct site visits, assess the merit of proposals, make recommendations to trustees, and process checks to recipient organizations. Throughout this process, grantmaking professionals work on behalf of boards that in turn owe some allegiance to the donor's intent. The twice-removed principal-agent relationship that lies at the heart of institutional giving creates the conditions under which grantmaking staff attempt to affirm process values—not substantive values—such as transparency, accountability, and fairness. The privileging of process is a natural function of professional staffers' attempt to discharge their duties with detachment and in a way that puts institutional interests first. While foundations all have donors in their past, the strength of an individual donor's values in guiding the institution tends to diminish over time, as the founder's vision is translated and interpreted by successive generations of agents, often first by family and friends, and then by persons who are increasingly distanced from the founder. While professional staff and outside directors may make every effort to respect the mission of the foundation as defined by the donor, this does not mean that the donor's values will be preserved over time.

One additional reason why many large foundations have gravitated away from the expression of the personal values and commitments of their donors can be traced to the way work has long been organized in foundations. Foundation staffers have never understood their work to involve expressing their own personal beliefs or values or even those of a donor they never knew. Rather, staff members see their work as involving the technical task of improving the foundation's effectiveness. As a consequence, passion and personality are rarely central to institutional philanthropy over the long run. This allows it to be cool and technocratic, and at times to achieve interesting results, but rarely does it startle or surprise with challenging and controversial philanthropic initiatives grounded in personal experience and strong value commitments. By focusing on developing coherent plans for the disbursal of funds, by choosing recipient organizations carefully, and by tracking results dutifully, program staff in institutional philanthropy are able to pursue at least one part of the core challenge of giving, namely, the achievement of instrument ends.

Over time, as donors leave the scene and as trustees and staff naturally take on greater responsibility for the disbursal of philanthropic resources, the capacity of institutional philanthropy to maintain a healthy balance between private values and public purposes is challenged. In the absence of clear and specific guidance from boards, staff struggle to interpret and act on the donor's intent, especially when it becomes difficult to ascertain the exact nature of the intent or to remain true to it as circumstances change and as time puts more and more distance between philanthropic principals and agents. In the end, the move to institutional philanthropy that many donors commit to when they form a foundation leads eventually to a kind of broad, detached, and technical form of philanthropy emphasizing instrumentalism over expressivism.

More Expressive Forms of Giving

For all the claims of the professional grantmakers to rationalize and normalize giving, large segments of philanthropy retain a strong emotive side. The trigger to giving is often the private passions and convictions of individuals. Drawn to philanthropy by a desire to do something significant that will give greater meaning to life, donors want their giving to reflect their values and identity. For younger donors, philanthropy can be a potent way to construct a public identity and to attach oneself to an issue or cause, a way to discover and manifest latent interests, or to engage in problems that otherwise appear too large or complex to tackle. For others, giving is a way to link private values and personal faith with real-world problems. Many small and large donors seek to make a statement through philanthropy, either to the public or to themselves about what they believe in and what their priorities truly are.

Not surprisingly, religious giving constitutes the largest share of all giving in the United States. It is animated and encouraged by faiths as diverse as Catholicism, Judaism, and Islam. Though usually small and local in character, faith has at times inspired large and ambitious philanthropy. One of the most far-reaching efforts to translate faith into philanthropic good works is that of Thomas Monaghan, the founder of Domino's Pizza. Monaghan was four when his father died, and two years later his mother placed him in a Catholic orphanage, where he was raised by nuns. Monaghan was an altar boy who considered the priesthood, but then drifted away from religion after joining the U.S. Marines and starting his pizza empire. He slowly became more and more involved in Catholic matters. He made a grant to an anti-abortion group that eventually led to a nationwide boycott of Domino's, and he funded the construction of a special chair for the pope to sit on while celebrating Mass during his visit to Detroit. Over time, Monaghan developed a close relationship with the Cardinal Edmund Szoka of Detroit, even underwriting a new computer system for the Vatican to help organize its finances when the cardinal was called on to help in Rome. However, it was only after Monaghan sold a large stake in his pizza chain for $1 billion that he began to give ever more aggressively and broadly. By putting $200 million into his Ave Maria Foundation and retaining plenty to donate directly, Monaghan's giving has spanned a range of activities—mostly with a conservative Catholic purpose. One grant that attracted controversy was a $2.5 million donation to support the construction of a large cathedral in Managua, Nicaragua, at a time when Monaghan worried about the spread of communism throughout Central America. While even his local priest urged him to find a way to use his wealth to help the poor with needed services, Monaghan's approach has consistently been to focus on the spiritual and moral lives of individuals.

Monaghan's Catholic philanthropy has been centered on higher education. One of his most ambitious undertakings has been the founding of the Ave Maria School of Law, located on Monaghan's office park outside of Ann Arbor, where the 270-acre headquarters for Domino's and surrounding office buildings are built in the style of Frank Lloyd Wright's Prairie School. Seeking to enact his faith and his belief in the importance of education, Monaghan's law school serves students who are interested in the moral dimension of the law and who have an interest in the intersection of faith and law. His critics contend that the law school is simply a tool for training the next generation of conservative lawyers who will go about trying to dismantle liberal jurisprudence. None of this concerns Monaghan, who has plans for a business school on the same campus.

Beyond starting this substantial undertaking, Monaghan has constantly sought out opportunities to fund projects that build spirituality. While other funders want to focus on critical material needs, Thomas Monaghan's philanthropy consciously focuses on faith. He even bought a fraternity house that was for sale on the campus of the University of Michigan, and after removing all the vestiges of party life and self-indulgence, converted the house into a dorm for Catholic girls, including crucifixes on the walls of every room. In addition, he has created several Catholic schools for girls that he believes make faith a more central part of learning than that of the existing Catholic schools. Monaghan's far-ranging but consistent philanthropy has not gone unnoticed. In fact, he is one of the most visible Catholic philanthropists in America, whose giving has earned him the privilege of taking Communion from the pope and having his daughter married in St. Peter's Basilica, with Cardinal Szoka presiding.

Other donors use their giving not to express their faith, but rather to honor what has meaning and significance to their lives. The case of David Duffield, founder of the computer software firm PeopleSoft, Inc., is a case in point. Duffield and his wife had a very deep and important relationship with Maddie, a miniature schnauzer that lived with them before their fortune was made. The dog was a profound source of happiness for the couple, who could not have children of their own. Maddie's strong personality and affection were important to Duffield as he worked hard to build his business. He pledged to the dog that if he ever made a large amount of money, he would give it back. Maddie died in 1997 of cancer after ten years with the Duffields, but the dog would not be forgotten. Duffield became a billionaire and made the largest commitment to animal welfare in history through Maddie's Fund: a $200 million endowment to support animal welfare and create a network of no-kill shelters.

Giving away millions a year to fund animal welfare proved difficult to do effectively. Duffield hired the head of the San Francisco Society for the Prevention of Cruelty to Animals (SF/SPCA), which operated the nation's largest and prominent no-kill shelter, to run Maddie's Fund. SF/SPCA's shelter was known nationwide as a model that provided great care to stray animals. Seeking to illuminate the practice of euthanasia in a country that annually puts to sleep 5 million cats and dogs in overcrowded shelters was an ambitious goal. However, drawing on experience in the technology field in which revolutionary ideas are regularly turned into successes, Duffield and his team forged ahead with their plan to offer grants to shelters that pledge to find homes for all animals within five years. Making grants that escalate as the shelters improve their performance, Maddie's Fund awards a $1 million grant when a shelter has fully reinvented itself into a no-kill facility that places all animals regardless of age, appearance, or physical disability. To achieve its goal, the fund also strives to reduce birth rates among animals and to ensure that families who have pets are able to keep them over the long run.

Some donors give because their memories are strong and philanthropy is a way to leave a visible imprint on society that is more lasting and universal than a personal recollection or private feeling. Mary Ford Maurer grew up in Kansas City. One of her fondest memories was going to Union Station to visit her father's office at the Fred Harvey Company, where he was secretary-treasurer. She would often go out to lunch with her father in the station, where the two would talk. Four children, ten grandchildren, and two great grandchildren later, she returned to Union Station for a hard-hat tour of the ongoing renovation. When asked to support the project, she offered $200,000 to pay for the renovation of the grand old clock in the station. Married to a successful businessman, Maurer ran the investment company for thirteen years following her husband's unexpected death at the age of sixty-six. She conducts much of her giving from a donor-advised fund in a community foundation and likes the fact that she can accumulate charitable assets in her account, save them for a major gift, and think about all the options before committing to efforts such as the clock restoration project. Other gifts by Maurer have been spread across the arts, education, and social services. Though not a member of the Community Christian Church, she was enraptured by its steeple of light, formed by light beams projected into the sky during weekends, and helped maintain it with a grant driven mainly by emotion and visceral attraction.

Charitable, instrumental, and expressive philanthropy can and do overlap with one another and create more blended forms of philanthropy. Moreover, few donors remain absolutely consistent across all their giving over time or even at any given point in time.

Donors may hold a diversified portfolio of philanthropic commitments that may include, for example, some local charity around the holidays, a few detached donations to worthy organizations with strong reputations, an expressive gift to their church, and, if they are thoughtful and deliberative, a few commitments that tend toward the more strategic, linking private commitments and significant community or public needs. There is also an evolutionary dimension to the four main forms of value creation in philanthropy. Donors who start out doing instrumental or expressive giving will often evolve their philanthropy over time into more strategic forms of giving as experience allows them to sharpen their focus and gain clarity of purpose. On the other hand, many of the most strategic grantmakers consciously allow themselves room to engage in more traditional forms of charity, when the circumstances call for it. As donors move in and around the matrix presented earlier, working within and between the forms and experimenting with different philanthropic tools and techniques, they sometimes achieve the kind of fit and alignment that is a required element of strategy.

Bringing It All Together: Strategic Giving

Giving that marries instrumentalism and expressivism is difficult to clearly delineate and can take many forms. It is not defined by the substantive issue that it happens to embrace, but rather by the quality of the fit achieved and by the melding of public purposes and private values. In formulating a grantmaking agenda, some donors attempt to both reflect the values that were important to the donor while producing broad benefits for the public. When successful, they come closest to approximating the interesting confluence of instrumental and expressive dimensions. One possible example can be found in a major philanthropic commitment made by the F.W. Olin Foundation. Over the years, this foundation funded the construction of over seventy engineering buildings on college campuses around the country to reflect the donor's abiding commitment to engineering education. Born in 1860, Franklin W. Olin received little formal education, but he was determined to study engineering and eventually graduated from Cornell University. Olin played in forty-nine games during two years of major league baseball with the American Association's Washington Senators and Detroit Tigers, but his engineering skills proved greater than his athletic ability. After designing textile mill machinery, Olin began to work on powder mill construction. Olin founded two munitions companies around the turn of the century that proved profitable. In 1938 he created the F.W. Olin Foundation to which he donated most of his fortune upon his death in 1951. Over the coming decades, the trustees of the foundation sought to honor Olin's dedication to science and engineering by making major grants to support the advancement of engineering education around the country.

In 1997 the F.W. Olin Foundation attempted to make an ever bigger impact on engineering education by creating the Franklin W. Olin College of Engineering, a new undergraduate school that would be located just outside of Boston. The foundation committed $300 million of its $500 million endowment to the effort, with the promise of more if needed. In a creative move, the foundation's board looked at a number of different undergraduate education models and found the Claremont Colleges' approach very appealing. Under this approach, a group of independent colleges shared major facilities such as a gymnasium and library while maintaining their own academic independence. The Olin Foundation eventually struck a deal with Babson College to purchase from the college seventy acres of land adjacent to its campus. The partnership was appealing to the board of Olin, because it would connect the engineering school to a college that has a national reputation through its business school for teaching entrepreneurship, something that well-rounded engineers eager to translate their ideas into products truly need, something that the donor understood and believed in deeply.

The new Olin College set out to break some old rules in higher education. Tenure is not offered to faculty. Instead, faculty members are given five-year renewable contracts based on peer review. At the time of the college's inception, students paid no tuition or room charges, and though the economic downturn has forced the college to change this policy for the 2010–11 academic year, all students continue to receive large merit scholarships. To attract the very best students, who otherwise might attend MIT or Caltech, Olin differentiates itself initially by offering full-tuition scholarships to all admitted students. To date, the college has successfully recruited many classes of students and continues to offer generous scholarships to all students. After receiving over a thousand applications for a maximum of sixty teaching positions, it has built a group of faculty committed to undergraduate engineering education.

How successful this risky and innovative philanthropic effort will prove to be will not be definitively known for many years, but the signs are encouraging. Olin has been repeatedly ranked as one of the top ten undergraduate engineering programs by *US News & World Report* as well as praised by other college-ranking publications. What is significant about it is the scope of its ambition and the fervor to enact the donor's values that mobilized the foundation's board to depart from their traditional grantmaking procedures that supported existing institutions. In this case, the board of the foundation decided to act in a way that a major individual donor might, by taking a substantial risk and investing in something that has a potentially high return rate. In seeking to develop a new model of undergraduate engineering education, the F.W. Olin Foundation has attempted to produce both expressive and instrumental value, and to satisfy both the intent of the donor and the needs of society for well-trained engineers.

Some donors are moved not by causes, but rather by a personal attachment to communities, and attempt to build a strategy for giving accordingly. Dean Mathey, a partner in the investment firm Dillon, Read & Co., created a foundation that would work to improve the small town of Grafton, Vermont. The Windham Foundation has three main goals: to restore historic buildings in the small town and to promote the economic vitality of the village of Grafton; to provide limited financial support to educational and charitable causes in the area; and to develop projects that will benefit the welfare of Vermont and Vermonters. These broad purposes have been pursued through an operating foundation, which uses the foundation's resources to both operate programs and to make some grants. Since its founding in 1963, one of the main accomplishments of the foundation has been the restoration of the grand old tavern and inn in the center of the village, which now hosts visitors year-round, and a collection of smaller buildings around the village that date back to the early decades of the 1800s. To preserve the character and integrity of the town, the foundation owns approximately 1,600 acres of land around the village. An interesting difference between Grafton and places such as Colonial Williamsburg, the historic village that is a museum, lies in the desire of the Windham Foundation to make Grafton a vibrant working community. Today the foundation employs around one hundred people in the various for-profit enterprises that it operates, including a sheep farm, a cheese factory, a nursery, and a ski center.

While donors may start with an issue or problem that they want to address or solve and then work to build a philanthropic response, Mathey's philanthropy started with a commitment to a village and a way of life. The village of Grafton faced problems of economic viability and historic preservation, but these social problems were not what animated the giving. Instead, it was the idea that a village was a special place that moved the donor to act and to seek to help. Using an operating foundation to restore and protect a picturesque village in the Vermont hills is certainly quite different from funding a program to assist the urban poor or preventing the spread of disease in a foreign land. It is a form of giving that starts with the experience and passion of the donor and then projects this feeling onto a broad public purpose, in this instance the preservation of rural Vermont's way of life and heritage. Mathey's use of an operating foundation was interesting because it signaled a more hands-on, local approach to giving, one in which the funding of programs would not be left to outsiders, but instead to enterprises controlled by the foundation and employing town residents. Given the needs of the town residents for stable employment and the desire of the donor to preserve the historic character of the town, it represented a well-aligned strategic choice, one that has served the town and the donor's vision well.

Although it is difficult to draw a clear and precise line in philanthropy between instrumental giving, expressive giving, and giving that blends the two together, what should be clear is that finding a synergistic point of contact between worldly effects and the personal beliefs of a donor can be understood as a continuum leading from less to more joint forms of value creation. Donors may not always want to produce joint value in their giving and may at times experiment with other forms of value creation. In the end, philanthropy needs to be understood as being about both the production of public benefits and the enactment of the donor's beliefs. While these may be accomplished separate from one another through serial acts of more or less instrumental and expressive forms of gifts, there is something powerful and compelling when both are part of a single philanthropic act. The power of strategic giving comes from the infusion of private visions of the public good into society, which can have significant and often unanticipated effects. Unfettered by the need to secure the support of others and capable of acting in ways that government cannot even contemplate, donors are in a position to bring eclecticism and innovation to the public sphere. How well and how responsibly donors grasp the opportunities available to them is a function of the quality of their strategic vision.

The capacity of philanthropy to bring these two elements of giving together—the private values of the donor and the public needs of the community at large—has been both challenged and renewed over time. As major donors have turned over their philanthropic fortunes to foundations and entrusted others to carry on their philanthropic legacy, the expressive content of philanthropy slowly but steadily dissipates from giving: boards turn over and become less and less familiar with the donor, and staff work diligently but ultimately seek to carry out their responsibilities, focusing often on honing the grantmaking procedures and ensuring that funds are used sensibly and for their intended purpose. This slow and gradual drift challenges the capacity of philanthropy to maintain the dual focus on private values and public purposes. But there are countervailing forces at work that are renewing the field. Every year new donors enter the scene and begin to project their visions of the common good into the public sphere. Sometimes they stumble and find that producing social returns through philanthropy is far harder than generating financial returns in the business world. Still, the field benefits from a constant flow of new donors who enter with fresh ideas and distinct assumptions. Whether the ossification that occurs in some parts of the institutional landscape of philanthropy is exactly offset by the infusion of new funds and ideas is impossible to know. What is certain, however, is that the field of philanthropy experiences regularly both the birth and death of expressive and instrumental forces. Somewhere in this complex process of transformation, all four main forms of value creation are pursued.

Decisions that donors make about the remaining four elements of the philanthropic prism will substantially impact the ability of donors to find the elusive point of overlap between instrumental and expressive giving. Settling on a good logic model, a sensible giving style, the right time frame, and an appropriate vehicle will all significantly affect the likelihood that the choice of value to be produced will turn out to be one that has strong strategic potential. Looked at from the other perspective, having a purpose that connects private passions to public purposes will not be in and of itself sufficient to overcome the many roadblocks that present themselves to donors seeking to achieve a greater level of alignment and fit in their philanthropic strategy. It does, however, constitute a necessary piece of the puzzle.

CHAPTER THREE

Logic Models: Theories of Change, Leverage, and Scale

As donors turn their attention to the world and seek to create value, they inevitably confront the question of how best to achieve their intended objectives. At the heart of this question is the idea of philanthropic effectiveness. Most donors, even those animated by values and the desire to express their convictions, are committed to doing so in a way that produces results. In searching for ways to give money effectively, donors have many options and confront a wide range of theories about how to achieve impact. It is possible to think about these theories as falling into three main categories: theories of change, theories of leverage, and theories of scale. Of course, there are strong connections linking these theories to one another, and choices made in one realm have consequences for choices made in others. All three pieces actually fit together into what is known as a logic model.

Elements of a Logic Model

A logic model (see fig. 3.1) can be understood as a formal explication of how a philanthropic intervention proposes to achieve its ends. Logic models can take the form of the specification of causal linkages,

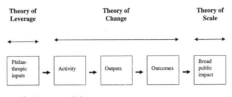

Fig. 3.1: Elements of a logic model.

which together articulate the steps that must be completed for an intervention to succeed. Sometimes logic models take the form of path diagrams with arrows connecting boxes, leading to the ultimate desired outcome. To construct a logic model, donors need to be clear about the ultimate goal or objective of their giving. Without clarity about outcomes, a coherent logic model is impossible. Donors also need to understand the starting point they are facing and the steps they will take along the way toward achieving their goals. One of the most common problems with logic models is the mistaken belief that they include all the relevant determinants in a causal chain leading from intervention to social outcome. In reality, the vast majority of social interventions have built within them a substantial amount of noise outside the system that affects the outcome. This large residual factor may well dwarf the programmatic elements in the logic model in terms of its relative explanatory power. Still, all donors, like all researchers, need to proceed in the face of substantial uncertainty about what statisticians call the residual problem. While not crippling to donors seeking to construct logic models in their chosen fields, the residual problem should at least be a cause for some humility and modesty.

Clarifying a logic model usually starts with defining a theory of change that commits the donor to a set or class of giving targets. Theories of change can be very broad and define the level—ranging from the smallest societal units to the largest ones—at which the philanthropy will work. At one end of this spectrum are theories of change that focus on the training and development of individual leaders who might someday transform a field of practice. At the other end are theories that seek to bring change by shaping public policy at the national or even international level. This hierarchy of change theories merely spells out for donors a set of initial choices about how to direct their giving at a particular unit of society. Choosing the right theory of change depends on a host of considerations, including the field in which the donor is working and the nature of the outcome that the donor is seeking to produce.

Theories of leverage are different from theories of change in that they focus not so much on the grand idea of how impact is best created, but rather on the mechanics of the process. Leverage is something that allows donors to increase the effectiveness of their giving. It is a concept grounded in the physical principle, familiar to many, that a long lever may be more useful than a short one in dislodging or raising fixed objects. When a lever is placed under an object and a fulcrum is located, the lever allows one to exert greater force on the object one is seeking to move or raise. The idea of giving grants and seeing—through the strategic construction of leverage—an impact greater than the amount of philanthropic funds expended has long been a powerful attraction to donors. As a consequence, many donors spend a fair amount of time experimenting with different philanthropic tools designed to create a greater impact. Not surprisingly, the need to achieve leverage in giving increases as the size of the social problem or issue the donors are seeking to address grows in size. The need for leverage also increases as the amount of philanthropic funds at the donors' disposal decreases.

Beyond developing a theory of change and locating points of leverage, donors concerned with increasing the impact of their giving tend to focus on a third element: the theory of scale that will guide their philanthropic work. While some donors are content with making small, targeted gifts designed to meet episodic needs, many donors want to see their philanthropic work broadened. A successful intervention, when properly understood and documented, can be brought to scale through a variety of means so that the number of people who are able to benefit from the program or intervention increases. For many donors, achieving scale represents the final piece in the operational puzzle that starts with the development of a change theory and continues with the pursuit of greater levels of philanthropic leverage.

Theories of change, theories of leverage, and theories of scale can be understood as a set of interconnected concepts, all pointing toward the idea of increased programmatic effectiveness and impact. Theories of change are the heart of logic models and strategy development. Theories of leverage and scale are the supporting tactics at the front end and back end of the logic model that allow the donor to maximize impact. Donors able to sketch out some clear notion of any of these three elements will be in a better position to maximize the public benefits of their giving. While there is no guarantee that getting better at giving will increase a donor's personal satisfaction, there is a large body of experience in philanthropy that suggests that donors who manage to achieve their objectives are often motivated to give more compared to donors who are thwarted in their efforts. For this reason, getting better at the mechanics of giving is an important element in the philanthropic prism.

Theories of Change

Theories of change operate at five distinct but interconnected conceptual levels: individuals, organizations, networks, politics, and ideas. At the individual level, many funders focus on training and developing people for leadership in fields where change is needed. Focusing on building skills and creating opportunities for individuals promises to create an army of change agents, ready both to change practice in the field and to lead efforts to change public policy. Important issues of independence and control arise when funders seek to change a field by training and developing new leaders. After all, the individuals taking part in such efforts need to be able to pursue their own goals. Still, many donors have attempted to walk the fine line between neutral professional development programs and initiatives that advance a fixed agenda through the cultivation of leaders. When done well, leadership development, training, and professional education programs can help build the human capital in a field, cultivate new skills, and motivate the people to continue working toward the missions that matter to them.

Training and developing people in a given field requires a long-term perspective, especially when the field already has entrenched leadership or when the field is young and still evolving. Often such efforts take the form of summer institutes, seminars, executive programs, distance learning, fellowships, sabbaticals, and other efforts to identify and encourage talented people to take on greater responsibility for shaping a field. For example, beyond the work of the Broad Foundation in the area of public school reform, several funders have sought to generate change by establishing a large selection of training and management programs for teachers, principals, and superintendents. By starting with individuals within a large and complex system, funders are making a conscious strategic choice, one built on the belief that broad change starts at the level of the individual.

Another way to bring change to a field is to create and support strong organizations. In the search for ways to build capacity within nonprofits, many foundations make an initial round of grants aimed at providing nonprofits with technical assistance, planning, and capacity-building advice—so as to position nonprofits to move ahead on a larger scale with their programs. Often this assistance takes the form of consulting on topics ranging from board development to marketing to capital construction. While some nonprofits bristle at any intrusion into their planning and operations, foundations often see capacity building as critical to positioning nonprofits to have broader influence and visibility. Working to support stronger organizations can be seen as a theory of change that prioritizes institution building as a critical ingredient in broader efforts to change a field.

Donors often wrestle with the question of whether their giving should focus on building the existing capacity within organizations or on creating new capacity, either in the form of new projects in existing organizations or through the formation of entirely new organizations. After all, sometimes existing organizations cannot be reformed through technical assistance or consulting. At one level, creating a new initiative or organization can be exhilarating. It offers the possibility of taking an idea from concept to reality, while shedding the baggage that almost all established organizations carry with them. Decisions about staffing have more flexibility when the organization chart is a blank piece of paper. Without a dominant culture or a set of standard operating principles, new nonprofits are free to either scan the environment and focus on best practices or to consciously seek to do things differently. Starting without a history also potentially opens the door for the donor to place a large and enduring mark on the organization.

Still, there are important drawbacks to starting from scratch that must be weighed. The nonprofit sector is rife with duplication and excess capacity. In almost every American city, multiple nonprofits do the same work. Often parallel projects proceed for years in total ignorance of one another, even if the target population is quite small. Rather than start new programs or organizations, many experienced donors believe that existing nonprofits need to be consolidated or, at a minimum, encouraged to collaborate more fully with one another. Accordingly, donors need to assure themselves that the new organization or project is really needed, and that existing efforts are simply unsalvageable or too costly to reform. The second drawback relates to operational efficiency: building something new will usually involve higher start-up costs and may in some cases require more time. Donors thus need to judge the cost and time delays that starting from scratch may bring against the benefits that come with such an approach.

Donors have also sought to create change by supporting collaborations and the creation of strong networks among organizations. The autonomous and disconnected character of large areas of nonprofit practice creates an opportunity for funders to have an impact. By locating groups with common values and goals, it may be possible to create a movement, or at least a coalition that did not previously exist. These networks can support the sharing of best practices, the pooling of resources, and the mobilization of advocacy efforts. Funding the creation of systems for collaboration appears to resolve some of the most glaring shortcomings in the nonprofit sector, namely, the duplication of effort and the inability to learn from others what works. Building networks of capacity within different fields promises to take small programs and local innovations to scale. By bringing people together and creating lasting networks of communication and collaboration, philanthropy is ultimately able to create the building blocks for broad movements and to overcome the isolation that many nonprofit organizations experience. Of course, networks of communication and collaboration can be transformed into policy and political movements when events create opportunities for action.

Another theory of change involves donors influencing politics. Philanthropy has attempted to shape policy through at least three different approaches. First, donors support projects that stimulate civic engagement by exposing citizens to politics and mobilizing them to take action. Often civic engagement is translated into direct political action by grassroots campaigns like voter registrations and other empowerment activities aimed at bringing the individual back into the public sphere.

Second, donors often ask nonprofits to play an important role in informing and educating the public and policy makers. Advocacy efforts take place at the local, state, national, and transnational levels, and often take the form of policy research and public information campaigns. Significant outlays of philanthropic funds have been made to support national advertising promoting reproductive rights, the dangers of tobacco, and other causes. Conservative foundations have famously invested heavily in public policy think tanks in their own effort to shape public priorities.

Third, donors make grants to nonprofits that engage in direct lobbying around specific legislative issues. Different from advocacy in its focus on specific bills of legislation, support of nonprofit lobbying is a way to translate philanthropic dollars into direct political action. While there are legal constraints on foundations when it comes to lobbying, individuals and corporations face few limits.

Working to shape the writing of a bill or to block the passage of one that is moving through the legislative process can be a potent and far-reaching intervention, particularly if the underlying legislation appropriates or denies substantial amounts of public funding for causes of interest and concern to the donor.

Beyond shaping politics and policies, donors can engage with problems at even higher levels of abstraction. They can support the production of new ideas and paradigms, which can reorient entire fields and lead to important breakthroughs in basic knowledge. Funding of basic research and theory building in fields as diverse as physics, geography, and economics can lead to new ways of understanding problems and seeing the world. If these new perspectives are able to penetrate the field broadly, they can usher in major changes that will have lasting effects not only on the further production of ideas, but on the way practitioners do their work. Being able to judge what constitutes promising and important research is a challenge, particularly because most funders are not that deeply enmeshed in the disciplinary debates across fields. For this reason, funders often ask other researchers to referee the applications submitted by their peers. Still, funding the production of transformative ideas is not easy to do well. Few outcomes of research can be predicted or expected, and there is no real guarantee that anything productive will result. Careful risk assessments would have probably made funding unlikely for many important breakthroughs, like those by Jonas Salk and David Ho. Despite the risks, with the right choice of author and topic, donors supporting the production of new ideas and concepts can generate significant change, whether by disrupting dominant assumptions or by catalyzing the reorganization of work to conform with a new understanding of the problem at hand.

The support for research can and often does intersect with politics. Funding policy research can have a tremendous impact when successful, as ideas from nonprofits filter through the public realm into politics. By funding efforts aimed at shaping both public and elite policy opinion, grantmakers can achieve substantial influence.

Informing policy debates in fields ranging from health insurance to welfare policy can turn modest philanthropic investments into major interventions in public life. For this reason, many funders see "idea philanthropy" as a far more potent tool for effectuating broad change than the incremental improvement of small segments of the service delivery system. The challenge of creating new and powerful ideas depends not only on being right, but also on finding ways to ensure that the ideas gain currency and infiltrate the political process.

UNRESOLVED ISSUES

If philanthropy does indeed operate across all five of the levels described here—including individuals, organizations, networks, politics, and ideas—there are at least two major questions that impose themselves, visible to all but not readily answerable by anyone. The first relates to the interaction of these levels. The second concerns the relative effectiveness of each of these levels. Neither question has been answered, nor even has been posed very clearly. Yet donors continue to struggle with the whole question of how to chart a change theory because the field has still not clearly defined its underlying assumptions and demonstrated the robustness of its causal claims.

At first glance, the five levels at which change is pursued in philanthropy appear to be neatly nestled, starting at the micro level of individual, moving up to the meso level of organizations and networks, and finally culminating in the macro level of politics and ideas. But the interactions among these levels likely are not linear and aggregating. In fact, many funders operate simultaneously and attempt to capture synergies across two or three levels. Foundations with multiple programs will typically identify for each field of activity a basic set of claims about the causal linkages they believe lead to the goals and outcomes they have defined. Within and across program areas, many if not all five levels of change will be pursued over time. The difficulty lies in specifying how these disparate attempts at driving change within and across fields add up to the kind of broad impact that donors usually aspire to achieve.

Beyond the uncertainty about the interaction of these levels, deep issues remain regarding the relative effectiveness of these approaches to driving change. It is hardly surprising that both risk and reward increase as one moves from small units of change (individuals) to much larger units (ideas). Beyond this bromide, the field of philanthropy lacks much basis for adjudicating between competing effectiveness claims related to change theories. While the largest foundations have hundreds of millions of dollars in grant funds available each year, many smaller donors, particularly those working outside the context of foundations, have modest resources. For these donors, knowing under what circumstances each of the five levels is likely to lead to the desired result is critical. Being able to bet correctly on advocacy work in one context, training programs in another, and network building in yet a third situation would allow smaller donors to apply their philanthropic resources efficiently and effectively. Unfortunately, information about the relative effectiveness of the five levels of change is hard to locate because few donors think in terms other than the tired dichotomy between direct service and advocacy rather than in this more differentiated way. Moreover, whether universal rules and dicta are even possible and what kind of data would be needed to create dependable knowledge are questions that remain unanswered.

In the absence of trustworthy measures of relative effectiveness of different change theories, the field operates based on what funders know. Even if program effectiveness could be gauged, it would be hard to establish the inherent superiority of any single change theory across contexts. As a result of this knowledge gap, individual donors and professional staff typically end up falling back on what they are most comfortable with. Funding political work is easier than funding basic research if one has years of experience in the world of public policy. Human nature simply guides donors to what they know and often makes it hard to break new ground.

Theories of Leverage

Donors have long relied on many different tactics to create change. All these tactics—in one way or another—aim at creating leverage. By leverage, donors usually mean a way of maximizing the impact of their contributions, ideally by creating significant activity or change with modest grant dollars. To do so requires turning grants from close-ended commitments into catalytic forces leading to greater productive work. Finding ways to achieve such results is important in philanthropy because the amount of money available to most funders is limited, especially when compared to the scope of human problems awaiting attention. Within the context of the needs and resources available, the idea of philanthropic leverage has understandably only gained greater appeal over the years. Even though huge amounts of money are at stake, philanthropy's "tool box"—its ideas about how to generate leverage—is surprisingly full of old, rusty, and blunt implements. What follows is a brief taxonomy of the most prominent tactics for producing philanthropic leverage that have emerged over time. These tactics are divided into two main categories: those that depend on the development of new grantmaking techniques and those that involve the construction of special kinds of interventions and programs.

GRANTMAKING TACTICS

In seeking to build leverage, foundations employ tactics that are centered on the nature and character of the grant itself. By adjusting the procedures and conditions connected to their grantmaking, many foundations believe they can achieve substantially greater impact and leverage. I focus here on five prominent grantmaking tactics that have at various times held out great promise for improving the ability of foundations to achieve change and impact. These include but are not limited to project grants; matching grants; loans and program-related investments; grants driven by proactive RFPs; and technical assistance, planning, and capacity-building grants.

Each of these tactics focuses on the grantmaking process, not the kind of program that is being supported.

Project Grants, Not General Operating Support
Leverage may be gained by increasing the control and oversight that donors are able to exert over donees. One strategy for control is the narrow circumscribing of purposes for which grants can be used. Many donors seek to target their giving to specific programs or projects within organizations, believing that these constraints make accountability, reporting, and assessment easier. By focusing grants on projects, donors are able to pick and support specific activities within an organization's portfolio of programs. Because of the possibility for greater accountability, donors generally believe that project giving is particularly effective. For nonprofits, the rise of project grants has been a mixed blessing. It has allowed proposals to be narrowly targeted and encouraged detailed planning. However, securing of unrestricted general operating support has become increasingly difficult. As more and more funders have sought leverage through project giving, some nonprofits have complained about the difficulty of sustaining core activities.

Matching Grants
One of the most obvious ways to create leverage is to make the receipt of a grant contingent on an organization's ability to raise additional funds. Matching grants can take many forms. They can require a one-to-one match, a three-to-one match, a five-to-one match, or any other ratio desired by the funder. Often matching grants are a critical part of large annual fund drives at major cultural institutions. Solicitations are made to individual contributors with the assurance that every dollar contributed will be matched and made to go further. For some donors, the existence of a matching program makes donating funds more appealing. Matching grant programs are premised on the idea that philanthropy can catalyze further giving by offering an incentive that increases the impact of additional fund-raising.

Loans and Program-Related Investments, Not Grants
Why give away money once and forever, when it can be loaned and recirculated over and over again? The starting premise of loans, be they for capital building or program expansion, is that leverage can be achieved by using philanthropic funds in a way that maintains grantmaking resources and allows for a much greater range of assistance being offered over the long run. Loan funds also build accountability and create a sense of responsibility that grants cannot duplicate. Program-related investments (PRIs) go one step further and attempt to achieve synergies between the investment needs of large institutional donors and their grantmaking objectives. By drawing on investment assets, PRIs achieve leverage by bringing endowment assets into the service of social objectives.

Grants Driven by Proactive RFPs
Many funders refuse to wait quietly in their office for the mail to arrive each day with requests for grants. While there is never a shortage of demands on donors, often the proposals that arrive over the transom disappoint, either in terms of subject matter or sheer coherence. As a result, donors have begun taking a more proactive stance when it comes to soliciting grant proposals. This sometimes involves contacting specific nonprofit organizations and encouraging the submission of the proposals, particularly if the donor has had a positive grantmaking relationship with the organization in the past. Other times, proactive donors simply open the door more widely through the creation of a request for proposal (RFP) that is advertised and open to any organization willing to deliver a proposal meeting the guidelines. RFPs spell out in great detail what the donor wants to accomplish and how the program should be carried out. Controversially, RFPs seem based on the assumption that the donor knows more about how to solve a given social problem than the service delivery community in the field. Given the pressure to be responsive, listen to needs, and "fund from the bottom up," RFPs and other proactive "top-down" approaches can ruffle some feathers.

Technical Assistance, Planning, and Capacity-Building Grants
Few nonprofits will ever admit that they are not "ready" to receive philanthropic resources or that there is a limit to their ability to grow. However, many funders have long believed that project grants alone do not lead nonprofits to plan and develop strategy and capacity. Therefore, before making large commitments, funders sometimes make an initial round of grants aimed at providing nonprofits with technical assistance, planning, and capacity-building advice—so as to position nonprofits to apply later for larger grants, or simply to move ahead on a larger scale with their programs. Often this assistance takes the form of consulting on topics ranging from board development to marketing to capital construction. While some nonprofits bristle at any intrusion into their planning and operations, funders often take an important step in making sure that this approach to leverage does not end up causing nonprofits undue concern: grants for technical assistance, planning, and capacity building usually leave the selection of the consultant or personnel to carry out the work in the hands of the nonprofit organization. When this simple step is taken to protect the autonomy of nonprofits from outside control, grantmaking aimed at assisting nonprofits to grow and develop capacity has a higher likelihood of being received positively.

PROGRAMMATIC TACTICS

A second set of leverage tactics is connected to the kind of program that is funded. These tactics aim to increase the effectiveness of grants by restricting the use of philanthropic inputs to a special class of activities. Though there are many more, I identify here five tactics that have either received substantial public attention lately or that have already channeled substantial philanthropic resources: support directed at specific geographical communities; support for nonprofit collaborations; private funding for public programs; support of commercial ventures within nonprofits; funding for organizations designed and set up by grantmakers. This approach to leverage begins to bleed into the theory of change, since all of these tactics focus on the kind of activity that is funded, rather than on the nature and terms of the grant itself.

Communities, Not Program Areas

Most foundations today organize their grantmaking around program areas such as social services, health, education, the arts, and environment, or narrower fields such as community development, early childhood development, and youth violence prevention. While foundations may focus on the needs of a city or state, most grantmakers think about their programs in terms of subject matter. Program staff are hired to work in substantive areas and are expected to become experts in their fields. A new theory of leverage has emerged recently to challenge this basic way of organizing philanthropic work. A few foundations have jettisoned traditional program areas in favor of a broad, cross-functional focus on specific geographical communities. The logic behind this move is simple enough. Problems are not categorical but dependent on a full range of interrelated issues within communities. By focusing on specific counties, towns, and city neighborhoods, funders believe that they can get leverage by focusing activity in confined areas. The move to geographical areas is intended to conceptualize social problems in a more realistic and holistic way. Rather than reify problems by categorizing them through traditional programmatic labels, this new way of thinking about grantmaking activities aims to achieve leverage through the coordination and concentration of effort.

Support for Nonprofit Collaborations, Not Isolated Work

Some foundations in recent years have seen a possibility for leverage through a return to early and once outmoded philanthropic ideas about one-stop shopping for social services—albeit now presented in the more fashionable language of collaboration and program integration. The fostering of collaboration among nonprofit organizations is appealing because the specialization of nonprofit services has made navigating the system increasingly difficult for many clients. To encourage collaboration, some foundations give preference to grant requests that include plans for cross-agency coordination. Leverage is achieved by reducing the redundancy and isolation of providers, and thereby improving the effectiveness of the entire service delivery system.

Private Funding for Public Programs
Not content with funding nonprofit organizations, a few foundations have begun to make grants directly to state and local government agencies. On the surface, such a tactic would appear to be "leverage free" given the ability of government to raise revenues through taxation. However, times have changed. Many state and local governments are strapped for cash and have little discretionary spending ability. Enter foundations offering grants with the stipulation that government carry on the program (birth control clinics in schools, for example) after the grant period is concluded. Significant leverage is achieved by locking government in to funding an activity that it receives for free for a short period of time. There are significant questions about democratic accountability related to these tactics, because they do appear to compromise local decision making. However, aggressive funders do not shy away from putting such conditions on grants to government, seeing an opportunity to press an agenda in the long run by funding it in the short run.

Funding of Commercial Ventures within Nonprofits
One of the most important changes in the nonprofit sector in recent decades has been the rise of earned income as a source of agency finance. Unlike contributed income, revenues from fees and ventures have no strings attached, and as such are attractive to many organizations. At the same time, funders have become aware of the entrepreneurial skills present in some nonprofits and have responded with an approach to building leverage that targets the commercial impulse of nonprofits. A growing number of donors now make grants to help nonprofits start or expand commercial ventures. While these activities are often substantially related to the

mission of the nonprofit, at times they are unrelated. By supporting a nonprofit's ability to generate a stream of commercial income,
funders gain significant leverage. Philanthropic funds are not only
converted into one-time programmatic activities, but instead they
are used to build income-producing capacity that will continue long
after the grant funds are gone. For nonprofits, an emphasis on commercial revenues is both potentially liberating and distracting. Run-
ning successful ventures demands staff time and resources. Still, the
availability of philanthropic funds to build capacity to move away
from a dependence on contributed income is a potentially empow-
ering proposition.

Funding for Organizations Designed and Set Up by Grantmakers
The continuous search for leverage has led a few large foundations
to take the drastic step of stepping outside the existing market of
nonprofit service providers in order to set up independent nonprofits to carry out the foundation's interest and agenda. Most often, the
decision to set up a new organization is related to an effort to shape
public policy, coordinate a group of existing organizations working
in a common area, or carry out some other function not directly
related to service provision. Few foundations explicitly set up new
organizations to compete with existing nonprofits. Instead, the leverage often comes from creating an umbrella organization that
meets a need not currently met by other nonprofits. Sometimes the
organizations that are started have a limited life, while other times
they evolve into enduring entities.

The obvious question that these varied philanthropic machinations
raise is whether any of these strategies and tactics, schemes and
dreams improve the effectiveness of giving and increase its social
impact substantially. The answer is, I believe, unclear. What is clear,
however, is that the greatest opportunity for philanthropic impact
has been neglected for way too long: philanthropy needs new basic
research on ways of generating change and achieving leverage. All of
which comes back to answering the not-so-simple question posed at

the outset: "How do donors have impact?" This is a question that is definitely worth *trying* to answer. The fact that the history of philanthropy has been filled with so many attempts at reform and renewal is both encouraging and depressing. While it is unlikely that any one of the theories of leverage described here has or will in itself transform philanthropy in the future, it is encouraging that donors in the past have worked hard to improve their giving.

Theories of Scale

Assuming that donors are able to create coherent and compelling theories of change and leverage to guide their giving, they are still left with the difficult task of building on proven successes so as to reach as many people as possible. Being effective means more than just carrying out an initiative well and meeting the needs of a small group of people. Effectiveness also involves reaching many people and taking the social leverage that an intervention creates and amplifying it even more broadly. Given the interest in having a real impact, donors speak variously of taking a program to scale, going to scale, and scaling up. What exactly is meant by scale? At its core, the idea of scale is focused on creating a lasting and significant impact. Beyond the broad idea of more or larger impact, scale has at least three core meanings in philanthropy, which are often collapsed in practice. Scale can refer to (1) financial strength, (2) program expansion, and (3) multi-site replication.

SCALE AS FINANCIAL STRENGTH

The first meaning of scale is related to organizational strength and sustainability. Large institutions such as museums and universities have achieved scale because they have visible institutional profiles and reputations for excellence across the nation, occupy large buildings or campuses, and possess the financial wherewithal to persist indefinitely. Scale on this account is equivalent to financial strength and sustainability, often secured by an endowment or by large operating budgets with dependable revenue streams. In a sector in which financial crises are commonplace, scale means being able to withstand the test of time by being big enough to ride out the storms. The number of nonprofits that have gone to scale under this definition remains small, and many are concentrated in a few categories of nonprofit activity.

In principle, there are very few obstacles to taking any single organization to scale. Though philanthropic resources are limited, if focused on a small number of institutions, they are now available to create a new cadre of very large and durable institutions. In practice, many of the organizations that have achieved financial scale have been and continue to be supported by individuals or family foundations with living donors. Many recipients of this sustained largesse, such as private colleges and cultural institutions, are the beneficiaries of support from elites and provide benefits to them in return. Interestingly, in the case of private educational and cultural institutions, it is often the visibility, prestige, and competition with other donors that encourages supporters to give, and give more, year after year.

Large private foundations do not seem to embrace this notion of scale as readily as individuals, though there are some notable exceptions to this. Picking any single nonprofit organization as the one that will be taken to scale may appear unfair and capricious. It implies that a single donor should be able to disturb the competitive landscape and decide who wins and loses in the nonprofit arena. While this may be precisely what an individual would like to achieve, few foundations want to be perceived as inequitable and heavy-handed. As a consequence, they shy away from tipping the scales completely in favor of one organization over another. Moreover, foundations may be less likely to bring an organization to scale because their interests are not in the organizations they fund per se, but in the specific programs and outcomes that these organizations deliver. The foundations have priorities that overlap somewhat with the agendas of nonprofit organizations. When these priorities change, funders can and do find new organizations.

Another reason that individual nonprofits are not often brought to scale through the infusion of large amounts of money may be connected to efficiency concerns. While giving a nonprofit the ability to withstand the vicissitudes of the nonprofit marketplace sounds reasonable, it may not be the most efficient way to use philanthropic resources. Endowments are often established with a projected 4 or 5 percent draw rate. Funding a large programmatic agenda from an endowment therefore becomes an expensive proposition. There is also the concern that taking a single organization to scale will eliminate the leverage that funders have over nonprofits, because the funds will free the organization from the usual relationships of dependence. After all, if a nonprofit has enough money to conduct its programs without the continuous input of new contributions, an important performance incentive may be removed.

SCALE AS PROGRAM EXPANSION

The second meaning of scale refers to the breadth or scope of service, usually measured by the number of clients served. Going to scale in this sense is thus roughly equivalent to program expansion and reach. When a pilot or project is launched, the goal is often to take it to scale by funding it at a higher level and by bringing the program to more people. There is a sense that a good program can never serve enough people. As soon as an initiative seems to achieve significant results, one of the first impulses of nonprofit managers and funders alike is to ramp up the effort and find a way to identify and serve more clients. In the past, the ultimate ambition has often been to get local, state, or federal funding after a launch with private money.

A number of powerful forces propel nonprofits and their funders toward program expansion. First, funding scale as expansion appears fair and equitable in that it rewards past performance. Funding decisions can be justified by the results that are actually achieved. Second, growing a program will allow it to achieve greater operational efficiency, as the *marginal* cost of administration decreases as the program expands. Third, this approach creates incentives for nonprofits to develop and deliver successful projects. If nonprofit managers know that funding to grow their programs is dependent on how well their programs work, they will work harder to make them succeed. Fourth, it allows funders and recipients to work together over longer periods of time than they otherwise might under typical project funding.

Nonprofit organizations are especially comfortable with the idea of scale as program expansion. It represents a natural way to evolve a nonprofit from a small community organization to one with a broader presence and impact. For nonprofit managers, aiming toward scale as program expansion is important. Growing programs is seen as equivalent to professional success and can be a key to advancement. Moreover, the financial incentives in the sector provide a strong correlation between budget size and salary, with managers earning more depending on the scale of the program they oversee. As both a signal of success and as a tool for advancement, scale as program expansion is thus attractive to many nonprofit organizations.

From the perspective of the funder, allowing an organization with a proven track record to expand its operations represents both a high return activity and a relatively low-risk proposition. After all, the nonprofit has already demonstrated its ability to implement a given program. All they are seeking is funds for program expansion so that they can do more of one particular activity. This is a proposition that can be considerably less risky than the design and creation of a new initiative.

SCALE AS MULTI-SITE REPLICATION

When a particular initiative or service model proves successful, many dissect the essential elements of this model in order to reconstruct the effort elsewhere with different personnel and under different circumstances. Replication is one way to achieve scale, a technique that has been tried and tested in the business sector over

a long period of time. Replication can proceed in two quite different ways: (1) within the organization through a set of more or less
closely linked chapters or through a franchise system linking independent organizations; or (2) outside the organization through
independent efforts to create similar programs.

The chapter or affiliate way of replicating services has proved
critical to the expansion of many of the older and more established
service organizations and civic associations. Opening chapters in
cities around the country enables an organization to achieve scale
quickly yet maintain some degree of control through centralization.
Often chapters are established in a hub-and-spoke arrangement, in
which funds and resources flow back and forth between the center
and the periphery. One obvious problem with this approach is that
uniformity and consistency across chapters is difficult to achieve.
Not surprisingly, one of the biggest questions that this approach
raises is the amount of autonomy that should be granted to the
chapters or affiliates. Some organizations have successfully implemented loose confederations, while others have long operated
tightly controlled networks.

The competing franchise approach to replication is based on the
simple assumption that once a model has been established, the real
work involves copying and multiplying the model in as many places
as possible. Franchising has become popular with younger social
entrepreneurs who see this model as providing swift action. By licensing a "brand," nonprofits can go to scale quickly. A key challenge of the franchise approach is locating skilled people who are
capable of taking a model into a new city or community and implementing it. The brand name must be protected by some form of
quality assurance. Achieving consistency and measuring quality are
both difficult propositions in the nonprofit sector, however.

There are some clear difficulties to both chapter and franchise
replication. Replication is not an approach that can easily be initiated or directed by funders. Although funders may be able to foster
some replication through the use of grants and incentives, most
externally directed replication efforts will struggle with the vast

unruly and idiosyncratic tide of nonprofit organizations that re-sist imitation and convergence. While some innovations and ideas have been replicated, large numbers of projects are unable to find any takers, even when they have shown great promise. Replication may rest on the shaky assumption that nonprofits are amenable to cookie-cutter duplication. Moreover, some funders who experi-mented with replication strategies discovered that some initiatives successful on a small and local scale defy replication when taken out of their initial contexts. This seems especially true when the nonprofit is working with disadvantaged populations, where trust and credibility are crucial.

Replication also ensues if the philanthropist creates a pilot or model program and then allows government or other funders to take the effort to scale. The philanthropist Eugene Lang, for example, had the novel idea of "adopting a class" of middle school students at the inner-city school he attended years ago. Lang promised all the students in one grade that if they worked hard and stayed in school, he would guarantee to pay for their college education. When the New York State legislature got word of this offer, it did not take long be-fore a scholarship program was devised for other disadvantaged stu-dents. This proved problematic. Critically missing from this public-sector imitation was the direct personal involvement that was a central part of Lang's innovative educational gift. Thus, while it is tempting to think that a replication model involves the simple multiplication of existing programs and institutions, in reality this process is more labor intensive. Embedded in many successful programs are the vision and commitment of an individual. When the program is replicated in other sites, this personal connection is often missing and the organizations may pass from being an ex-pression of one person's values and beliefs to a more instrumental attempt to produce certain public benefits.

Although many funders like the idea of "going to scale," the num-ber of initiatives accomplishing scale under any of the three defini-tions remains small. Only around 200,000 nonprofits out of some 1.5 million have revenues above $25,000. The number of very large and successful nonprofits is considerably smaller than 100,000 and probably closer to 10,000, the majority of which are universities and hospitals. The achievement of scale thus raises a number of questions: When and why should any of these three different scale strategies be applied? Why does scale sometimes fail? Does the ideal of scale fit better in the business sector than in the nonprofit sector? Can commitments to scale and equity be embraced simultaneously? Are the less successful attempts at scale simply examples of domains in which public policy should be allowed to operate? Most of these questions remain unanswered even though scale has become a major target of organized philanthropy. Rather than engage these difficult questions, it is far easier to simply fall back on arguments about spreading the benefits more broadly and achieving efficiencies.

The fundamental problem with the concept of scale, as understood in the philanthropy field, is the assumption that the scope of public impact achieved through philanthropy correlates with the public value created. Scale seems an obviously desirable objective by virtue of the underlying math, namely that assisting 10,000 clients, all things being equal, is better than assisting 1,000. This assumption is particularly hard to defeat in the context of philanthropy because quality of nonprofit programs is difficult to measure. Using size as a proxy for impact is easy, as is embracing the idea that programs serving large numbers of people are contributing more to public welfare than those targeting smaller populations. But scale is not a particularly good proxy for effectiveness, and many large programs do not deserve the support they receive, while many smaller programs deserve great acclaim. When scale is pursued without adequate evidence of efficacy and without sufficient quality controls, it can undermine the coherence of a logic model. Guarding against this kind of misapplication is thus critically important in seeking to bring strategy to giving.

While a theory of scale typically comes toward the end of the process of perfecting a logic model, it should be conceived, along with a theory of change and a theory of leverage, as part of an in-

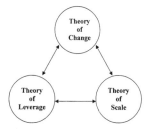

Fig. 3.2: Three elements of a philanthropic logic model.

tegrated system aimed at producing significant social impact. One way to visualize this system is to move away from the linear representation of the value chain in philanthropy presented earlier and toward the image of a triad, one in which all three elements are connected to one another (see fig. 3.2).

As donors look out across the philanthropic landscape at its abundant opportunities, many will want to include in their fundamental logic model a theory of change, a theory of leverage, and a theory of scale. These three conceptual elements can be a focusing device to help donors understand and render explicit some of their assumptions about giving. At the same time, no universally applicable or successful theories of change, leverage, and scale exist. Depending on the issue or field within which the donor is operating, and contingent on the choices that the donor makes in other parts of the philanthropic prism, choices vary considerably in ability to produce social benefits. Donors who attempt to take a logic model from one field and impose it crudely on another will be sorely disappointed. The context is critical in determining not only the logic model, but all the other elements of the philanthropic prism.

In the end, the real justification for a powerful logic model is not just its ability to provide the framework for evaluation, but also for donors to render clearly in their own minds their objectives for giving. The formalization of the donor's beliefs and assumptions through the construction of a logic model is a meaningful step on the road toward greater strategic clarity. In some sense, the quality

of thinking that lies behind giving and the plausibility of philanthropic intentions is as important as the eventual impact. A logic
model can be a telling representation of the donor's best judgment.
The care with which a donor disburses philanthropic funds is something over which donors have complete and absolute control and
for which they should be held accountable.

CHAPTER FOUR

Giving Styles

If philanthropy were purely science, then the task of the donor would be largely a technical one, consisting of learning the rules and laws governing giving, studying the key tools and systems needed to get from charitable intent to desired social results, and then simply applying all this knowledge to the resolution of human hardships. This is obviously not the case. And the field of philanthropy is better off because this is not the case. Philanthropy cannot be reduced to a narrow set of technocratic directives or even to a single set of prescriptive claims. In its natural form, philanthropy is full of art and personality, bursting with idiosyncratic visions, unsupported claims, and deeply held passions. The great mistake that many donors have made is to aspire to turning their giving into something purely efficient, precise, and consistent. The impulse to strive for a more scientific approach has been aided and abetted by the rise of a class of professional grantmakers in the foundation segment of the field, who have sought to normalize and rationalize giving. In the vast majority of large private foundations, the donor is no longer living, and the professionals carrying out the grantmaking do not feel authorized to insert their own values, but instead attempt to interpret fairly and neutrally the mission that has been given to them—all with an eye to maximizing public benefits. One of the recurring themes in this book has been that professionalization in philanthropy saps giving of the critical expressive dimension that makes the sector an original contributor to the public debate. Not all of philanthropy has been neutralized and homogenized. The many purposes pursued by individual donors and the multiple logic models they concoct are testament to the field's capacity for pluralism and diversity. No part of the landscape of philanthropy is as diverse as the giving styles of individual donors. The history of American philanthropy is full of colorful characters including religiously motivated helpers, politically connected operators, scoundrels from the world of business and finance, unapologetic egomaniacs and self-promoters, safety-seeking incrementalists, restless social innovators, and quiet but curious thinkers. Although it would be tempting to believe that the act of giving cleanses and reinvents those who choose to engage in it, in reality philanthropy more often than not simply magnifies and transposes the personal characteristics of the donor into a new and usually more public domain. Philanthropy brings out the latent personality traits of individuals and provides a channel to connect commitments to causes.

Two key dimensions of any individual's giving style are the level of engagement or involvement of the donor and the desired public profile. Before, during, and after funds are conveyed by donors to recipient organizations, a core challenge in philanthropy involves coming to an agreement about the ultimate purpose that both sides to the philanthropic exchange have in mind, a purpose that may represent the amalgamation of many, if not all, of philanthropy's complex functions. While the donor holds many of the cards in this game, recipient organizations are in a position to assert at least some control over the process. In this negotiation, donors are required to make important choices about how much engagement they want to have in their giving and how much public profile they desire. No matter why a donor gives, the act will demand that answers be given to how exactly the gift will be made and how philanthropic intentions will be translated into action. In important ways, the engagement and profile of donors will be shaped by the motives that lie behind the gift. If all a donor wants is to do some good, the profile sought will be low and the level of engagement will be appropriate to the project at hand and subject to joint definition by both sides of the philanthropic transaction. If, on the other hand, the donor has strong views about either engagement or profile based on personal considerations that have little or nothing to do with the actual project, problems are likely. A key element of good strategy thus comes down to calibrating the appropriate level of engagement and profile in one's giving.

Engagement

In assembling a plan for giving that includes an engagement strategy, donors need to think carefully about the question of who will carry out their philanthropic work and how. In some cases, donors will seek out the advice and counsel of family members, friends, lawyers, and consultants when executing their giving. These parties may be brought in to assist with planning or implementing a philanthropic agenda. A trend toward philanthropic disintermediation has, however, emerged in recent years: younger donors increasingly cut out all philanthropic middlemen and instead look to themselves as the principal agents of their own philanthropy. This do-it-yourself turn is, of course, the simplest solution to the agency question in philanthropy, one that removes the threat of deviation from the donor's intent that delegating responsibility can create.

Engagement styles range from very hands-off approaches, in which nonprofit autonomy and expertise are privileged, to more deeply engaged approaches, in which the donor and recipient work together on program development and problem solving. Some donors are involved in all aspects of their giving and the work of the organizations that receive their funds. Often stemming from a sense that philanthropy must be about more than check writing, involved or engaged donors want to feel a connection and offer advice and input above and beyond funds. So as to understand the community better, donors may talk to and toil alongside the inner-city community activists as they weed out a plot in the community garden. Donors may listen in on a board meeting of an organization that is attempting to overcome a challenge and offer suggestions where appropriate. Donors may introduce independent evaluators regularly into the program to advise both the organization and the donor on the strengths and weaknesses of the program design and implementation. There are many ways that donors can do more than just send checks. Two important questions are why do donors at times become engaged, and how do they go about adding value through engagement?

Why would a donor seek a high level of engagement with a recipient organization, rather than simply maintain a more traditional and distanced philanthropic relationship? The high-engagement donors may get involved because they want to help others to help themselves and gain independence. Or they may seek a high level of engagement simply because they believe that they know better than others how to manage a project, even if they lack the specialized training and experience of the leaders within the recipient organization. This impulse to micromanage and meddle can be a product of years of managerial work in the business sector, which may have led to substantial wealth creation and success. It is often just a small—though sometimes unwise—leap to assume that these patterns will lead to success in philanthropy. It is also possible that the drive to engagement can be related to vanity, overblown self-confidence, or a desire to impose their will on others.

On the other extreme, an increasingly smaller number of donors are happy to withdraw from the grantmaking process and to let recipient organizations do their work as they see fit. Such deference may stem from a recognition that in many cases it is the nonprofit that truly understands the problem at hand. It can also be the painful result of experience in attempting to be highly engaged, leading only to the recognition that nonprofit managers prefer to have plenty of leeway in how they operate their programs. Low engagement has also been justified in the name of professional detachment and as a necessity for maintaining objectivity. It is also far easier and less time demanding to limit the scope of the giving relationship to pre- and post-grant evaluation, rather than to expect the donor to take partial responsibility for the execution of a program or for the recipient organization's performance. In fact, the more engaged a donor is with a project, the harder the relationship may be to terminate, if the facts so dictate. Engagement can muddy the philanthropic waters by placing the donor into the program that is being funded, a position from which it is hard to render tough and objective judgments about quality and impact. For this reason, in some cases donors need to actively resist the temptation to throw themselves into the fray and get their hands dirty.

As they become more and more comfortable with giving, donors come to define for themselves an engagement style that fits somewhere between totally hands-off to deeply engaged. For nonprofits, these decisions about style can have significant consequences. High levels of donor engagement may mean access to resources and talents of great value to the nonprofit. It may also entail a tremendous amount of extra work, as donors need to be handled and satisfied. For this reason, some nonprofits prefer to receive general operating support with as few strings attached as possible. Over time, however, almost all nonprofits learn to work with the different engagement approaches of their donors and understand that considerable variation is to be expected.

The level of engagement will vary not only based on the style of the donor but also on the nature of the work being carried out by the recipient. Some work, such as scientific research or the arts, makes it hard for donors to be engaged directly in the funded work because it simply requires a certain amount of independence. Other kinds of projects, such as youth programs and scholarship funds, are more open to donor involvement and even reengineering. After all, everyone has an opinion on how to help young people, but few people know enough about genetic research to get deeply involved.

Besides the donor's desired level of engagement, the overall character of philanthropic engagement will also depend on the level of congruence or match between the values and intentions of the donor and the recipient. In some situations, donors and recipients think alike and share common aspirations, while in other cases, the two parties are very far apart, even if this is not apparent at the time of the grant. In either event, it is possible to view congruence, overlap, and coincidence in outlook and underlying values between donors and recipients as central to the formation of a strong working relationship. When these two dimensions are joined, four types of philanthropic relationships emerge (see fig. 4.1): contractual relationships in which donors and recipients simply give and get under narrowly circumscribed terms and then go their own way; delegating relationships in which donors delegate responsibility freely to those doing the work; auditing relationships in which trust is low and oversight is extensive so as to monitor the precise use of grant funds; and, finally, collaborative relationships in which the two sides work together closely to achieve a set of mutually agreed-upon goals.

What do these different engagement strategies look like in practice? When writer James Michener came to Texas in the early 1980s to research the novel he was writing that would eventually bear the state's name as its title, he was given tours of the biggest ranches, an office at the University of Texas, and special attention from the governor. Michener came to love the state and bought a house in Austin. He volunteered, in his words, as a "teaching assistant" in the graduate fiction workshops at the university. Michener worked closely with students, commenting on their work, encouraging when necessary, and giving them career advice. In 1988 he gave $1 million to create an interdisciplinary master of fine arts degree at the university, which would provide students with training in fiction writing, poetry, playwriting, and screenwriting. The goal of the programs was to develop multi-dimensional graduates who could work across a range of writing professions. Michener was not an absentee donor. Instead, he worked with the students and helped set the direction for the center. Within a couple of years, he made another gift of $3 million, followed by a $15 million contribution

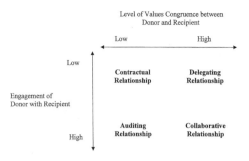

Fig. 4.1: Forms of philanthropic relationships.

to fully fund the new James A. Michener Center for Writers at the University of Texas, including fellowships for writing students. Michener was very involved with the program until his death in 1997. Collaborative relationships involve not only the gift of money but working together based on shared values and mutual interests.

Many gifts move away from deep personal engagement to a delegating relationship, in which values are aligned, but the donor does not have the time or inclination to get involved in operational details. One of the largest gifts ever recorded fits this description, and it turned out to be also one of the most controversial. Media mogul Ted Turner shocked many when he announced that he was giving $1 billion to the United Nations over ten years. The gift provoked both admiration for its size and ridicule for focusing on an agency that some argued had a reputation for bureaucratization and inefficiency. Still, for Turner, the gift represented a fulfillment of his commitment to international cooperation. For years he had flown the UN flag above the offices of CNN and had sponsored the Goodwill Games at a time when international tensions were running high. After its initial announcement, Turner's gift went through a number of changes. First, Turner created the nonprofit UN Foundation to receive some of the shares of Time Warner stock he acquired following the sale of the TBS company. Legally, the UN Foundation was not a foundation, but rather a public charity that would solicit outside funds to help support its activities. The gift was not limited only to the United Nations but was also directed at "UN causes," which include the UN Commission on Human Rights, a range of nonprofit environmental and advocacy organizations. The exact amount of the gift would also depend on the performance of Time Warner stock and would be capped at $1 billion, less if the stock performed poorly. Regardless of these changes, the gift sent a major shot across the bow of philanthropy by virtue of its size and ambition. To run the UN Foundation, Turner chose former U.S. senator Timothy Wirth, an experienced actor in international politics. Interestingly, Turner pondered a different use of his philanthropic funds before settling on the UN Foundation: he inquired into paying off the UN membership dues of the United States, which were in arrears, but decided against it.

At the other extreme of engagement approaches are donors that do little other than monitor progress, review financial statements, and ensure that the terms of the grant agreement are fulfilled. Depending on how closely values are aligned, this can produce a respectful contractual relationship or a more tense auditing relationship. These auditing models often arise in smaller foundations, where large numbers of small grants are made. Unable to do more than monitor grantees, these under-resourced foundations set a group of procedural hurdles in place designed to maintain some semblance of accountability. Nonprofits must submit to these periodic audits and remain in compliance. Monitoring financial matters is easier than monitoring mission fulfillment, and much of the auditing in philanthropy looks at accounting for and expending funds.

Contractual relationships are frequent in the world of corporate philanthropy, where gifts are conveyed often with relative detachment, but where there is some assumption of alignment between values—or at least interests. Companies that give are reluctant to get too closely connected to the organizations they support for a range of reasons. Chief among them is the fear of exposure to negative publicity should charitable programs backfire or fail. While executives may want to see their employees involved in community volunteer projects aimed at rehabilitating buildings or cleaning up beaches, they may not want to get too deeply involved in designing a community program aimed at tackling a tough problem such as crime or drug abuse. Moreover, the focus on the arts funding that is often present in corporate philanthropy makes engagement more difficult, because there are few real opportunities for company executives to help design an exhibition or a theater production—although there are ample opportunities at each to fly the corporate banner. The engagement level of corporate donors is generally lower compared to other donors for another reason: few company foundations have large enough staffs to really do more than process requests and focus on making sound grant decisions. Real engagement requires a substantial commitment of time, resources, and people, which are not always available in the context of corporate philanthropy. Many corporate giving programs are designed more to enhance company profile and recognition than to intervene in the work of nonprofits.

Engagement is a critical part of the style defined by a donor. It has implications not only for the overall fit and alignment of the giving strategy, but also for the nonprofit organizations on the other side of the table. Like many other elements in the strategic puzzle of philanthropy, engagement levels are variable and contextually defined by the interplay of public purposes and private values. Engagement is something that must neither be declared by donor fiat nor postulated by a recipient. Instead, engagement needs to emerge from communication between the two parties and should aim toward finding a level of fit and alignment that will satisfy both sides of the philanthropic exchange.

Profile: Anonymity and Acclaim

The second element to the idea of a giving style is the donor's profile, or the issue of when, whether, and how, if at all, to assume a public profile in philanthropy. This means carrying out a philanthropic agenda in such a way that it projects an image to the public about the donor, preferably an image of the donor that reflects well. Philanthropy attracts two extremes—and everything in between—

when it comes to profile: those seeking anonymity and those seeking acclaim. Just as with engagement, there is a broad distribution of styles. Some donors believe in the importance of a highly visible public profile, if for no other reason than to publicize the organization supported and attract additional funding. For every donor angling for media attention and recognition, there is a donor who prefers to maintain a very low profile and do most giving quietly and without much fanfare. For these givers, public attention given to the donor only risks wasting precious resources and diverts attention from the underlying mission and cause. Although personalities will dictate to some extent how much of a public profile a donor wants to assume, the comparative scarcity of anonymous giving suggests that donors usually want some kind of recognition and profile. Striking the right arrangement can test a nonprofit's ability to read and respond to the funding environment. This can be a complicated task since donors may want plenty of recognition but not want to ask their recipient organizations to provide it. In such cases, it falls upon the nonprofit to "read" the donor.

While engagement connects the donor to a nonprofit organization in ways that can be either productive or destructive, profile has less transparent and immediate implications. Recognizing a donor may not "cost" a nonprofit much, at least as long as the demands are modest and the donor has not been engaged in any activity that reflects badly on the recipient institution. In some cases, though, donors have had their gifts returned because of scandals, including at a university that named its convocation center in honor of its chief donor and only later learned he was a central figure in international arms dealing. Donors may request that their names be included in lists, honor rolls, and commemorative plaques, or they may want to be mentioned in press releases, advertising, and other outreach efforts. In all this jockeying, to please contributors and encourage them to give more in the future, some valuable resources may need to be diverted from mission-related work to donor satisfaction work. Still, there is at least one troublesome element in all of this. When donors decide to go public and seek to cultivate a public profile connected to their philanthropy, questions will always lurk related to motives. Of course, visibility can be defended on a number of strategic grounds, particularly for new funders who are eager to announce their presence to the broader field and for already well-known donors who choose to work in new areas that are still unknown to the public. High profiles can shed light and attention. However, concerns over ego and ambition will lurk nearby.

The drive for a high philanthropic profile can sometimes be the product of a desire to escape an existing identity and to change public perceptions. For some married women, high-profile philanthropy is a way of defining themselves and creating some separation from the long shadows cast by their husbands. Such was the case with Sheila Johnson. Within the span of one year, Sheila Johnson divorced her husband, split with him a $1.5 billion windfall from the sale of the television network they co-founded, Black Entertainment Television (BET), and moved to Middleburg, Virginia, with her two children to start a new life. Johnson soon made a number of significant donations and has plans for a $100 million foundation to pursue her philanthropic vision. Johnson established herself as a leading citizen of Middleburg just by buying a vulnerable piece of property. The mayor and many longtime residents were relieved when she bought a 342-acre estate previously owned by Pamela C. Harrison. There were fears that the estate would be converted into unattractive subdivisions, but Johnson declared her intention to turn the entire estate into a high-end lodging called Salamander Inn. She also underwrote lavish fund-raising galas for the Loudoun Hospital Center's health vans, which travel to the underserved pockets of her adoptive county, and gave $2.5 million for a performing arts center at the Hill School, a private school where her son is a student. The style of Sheila Johnson's giving is intertwined with her own personal goals and is, at least partially, a function of a drive to distinguish herself from the business she and her husband created. She has also used her influence to make a connection at Parsons the New School for Design and has been actively involved with the school's governance, serving on its board. Her involvement with

Parsons may be fueled as much by a desire to break into the fashion and design industry with her new business venture in fine linens as it is by a desire to get more philanthropic visibility. Nevertheless, Johnson's search for a new identity and the role philanthropy has played in the process are significant because they demonstrate how giving can transform the donor and not just the recipient.

Donors have at times sought to remain anonymous. For many reasons, anonymous giving is a special case in philanthropy. By giving anonymously, donors are foreclosing any "return" other than the personal satisfaction that arises from doing a good deed. Anonymous giving is a subject that is difficult to research and explore in great detail precisely because it is done anonymously and often with little public recognition. An example of this rare form of giving is useful, if only for contrast with the more dominant, higher-profile approach embraced by modern donors.

The most "famous" anonymous donor is Charles Feeney. This unassuming New Jersey man quietly gave away hundreds of millions of dollars before anyone knew he was the donor behind a Bermuda-based foundation. His veil of secrecy was pierced only when the sale of his company forced him to go public. Feeney created Atlantic Philanthropies from the proceeds of the sale of the duty-free business he created in airports. The foundation's assets have been declining lately due to Feeney's decision to spend his multibillion-dollar foundation out of existence over the course of a decade and a half. Uncomfortable with donors who fail to take responsibility for their own charity, Feeney's approach to giving while alive is anchored in the simple notion that money spent solving human problems today is better spent than money given away in the distant future. Moreover, giving while alive ensures that the donor experiences the pleasure of seeing good work done with their philanthropic funds. Brought up in a working-class neighborhood in Elizabeth, New Jersey, Feeney attended Cornell on a GI scholarship and studied hotel administration. The breakthrough for Feeney came when he and a partner opened duty-free shops in Honolulu and Hong Kong, then expanded around the world to capture growing tourist travel. Feeney's share in the business became worth over a billion dollars, but he had transferred his interest to a foundation in Bermuda called Atlantic Philanthropies. To avoid detection, Feeney chose not to claim a tax deduction. Part of his decision to maintain a low profile stemmed from his desire to live a normal life and not create security problems for his family. Atlantic Philanthropies' giving has spanned a range of issues, including improving the quality of higher education in Ireland, the support of nonprofit infrastructure organizations in the United States, and health programs in countries around the world.

Philanthropic profile is an element of strategy that can be managed, but only to a small extent. There are times when profile simply is determined by others. In New York, a taxicab driver decided to use the money he earned in the United States to engage in philanthropy back in his hometown of Doobher Kishanpur, India. By contributing $2,500 a year, Om Dutta Sharma is able to run a school for girls in the small house where he was raised. Because teachers earn only about $50 a month, Sharma is able to educate almost two hundred girls in grades one to five. His plans for the expansion are keyed to the sale of his taxi medallion when he retires from his regular driving schedule of twelve hours a day, seven days a week. Sharma's decision to give back in India was fueled by two major factors. First, he wanted to do something to honor his illiterate mother, so he named the school after her. Second, he realized that he did not have the funds needed to make a major difference in the United States. However, his modest contributions could go a lot further back in India. Thus, Sharma took the unusual step of applying his modest philanthropy to a place where it could create maximum impact. He did not seek any real public recognition for his giving. However, he was the subject of stories in the major media and was thrust into a highly visible position.

There are many donors who want to be acknowledged and thanked for their gifts, sometimes in very public ways. In fact, visibility can be a critical factor driving some donors' giving. The range of ways in which donors seek a public profile is broad, from having buildings named after themselves, to the hiring of public relations firms, to participating in special events to celebrate and recognize their gifts. Exacerbating this inclination is the fact that changes within the field of professional fund-raising have turned donor relations and donor acknowledgment into an increasingly elaborate and extensive activity. Structuring a giving opportunity so as to meet the profile desires of the donor is now routinely part of the process of securing a major contribution. It is not uncommon for donors to be approached about gifts with an explicit menu of "naming opportunities" and a clear offer of quid pro quo. However, when giving turns into a simple exchange of money for visibility and publicity, something important about philanthropy is threatened, namely, the balance between private and public priorities. The search for recognition and public profile can go too far and move philanthropy into a position in which the primary element driving giving is the private satisfaction of the donor, not the search for creative solutions to public problems.

Where do philanthropic styles, which include both a desired engagement level and a preferred public profile, really come from? They tend to be a product of the life experiences of the donor before philanthropy, rather than the result of a careful consideration of the strategic considerations at hand for any particular gift or series of gifts. Style is more fixed than other elements of the strategic framework. Yet the selection, testing, and adaptation of a distinctive philanthropic style for giving still require continuous reevaluation and adjustment in order to achieve a level of fit and coherence with the other elements of the "philanthropic prism." Engagement level and profile need to be flexible and able to adapt to the distinctive demands of specific circumstances, even if changes in style are personally difficult for the donor to make. The style adopted by the donor must meet the dual test of adding value to the philanthropic effort in question while also producing the kind of personal satisfaction that leads the donor to continue to give. Striking the balance thus requires a considerable amount of introspection and knowledge of the funding environment. New philanthropic fashions and trends can disrupt the process and make particular styles appear appealing. Unfortunately, style alone can never be a substitute for good strategy, only an element of it.

A New Style: Venture Philanthropy

One of the most popular styles in philanthropy in recent years has been one that transposes elements of the hard-nosed businessman or investor into the softer world of nonprofit activity. Donors have embraced the idea that significant value might be added if the philanthropic relationship between grantmaker and grantee is refashioned to look more like the relationship between an investor and an investee. Rather than simply being a purveyor of charitable funds for deserving organizations of all sorts, venture philanthropy promised to turn donors into hard-nosed social investors by bringing the discipline of the investment world to a field that had for over a century relied on good faith and trust. Yet while business firms had a clear way of determining whether their investments pay off—namely, return on investment—philanthropy has long struggled to develop performance measurement tools to assess the impact of philanthropic investments. Moreover, philanthropy struggles to marshal enough resources to have a major impact. The search for solutions to the problems of impact and measurement has been at the center of the conversation about venture philanthropy, as the approach has taken hold and begun to spread, especially among younger donors who have made their money through entrepreneurship. The attempt to transfer wisdom across sectors galvanized a small group of individual and foundation donors who have now declared themselves to be "venture philanthropists."

The impact of venture philanthropy has been broad. Though the exact size of the venture philanthropy movement today is difficult to pinpoint, one recent survey estimated that there are some forty institutional funders deeply committed to the approach, investing about $60 million a year. Although venture philanthropy remains small today, particularly when compared to the total $200 billion given away each year by all donors, its influence is considerable. The idea of turning philanthropy into social investing has been tried in a whole host of fields such as early childhood health, environmental protection, and community development, to name just a few. Venture philanthropy has been the subject of growing media attention, and the profiles of its early practitioners have risen within the field. Most significantly, several of the largest foundations, such as the W.K. Kellogg Foundation and the Pew Charitable Trusts, have recently begun to experiment with the language and practices of venture philanthropy. Therefore, it is critical to understand what the approach has to offer philanthropy.

At its core, venture philanthropy can best be viewed as being built on three main intellectual pillars, each of which is seen as a solution to a problem in traditional philanthropy. The first idea is bringing nonprofits to scale through the provision of large blocks of financial support to nonprofits over longer periods of time. The second idea is the development of new metrics to measure organizational performance. The third is the establishment of a close relationship between funder and recipient, one in which the donor engages with core strategic and operational issues and seeks to act as an advisor and problem solver for the organization. All three together constitute a distinctive style, one in which both engagement and profile are high.

Venture philanthropy has developed tools aimed at increasing the likelihood of success in nonprofits, including the provision of a different kind of capital flow than nonprofit organizations are used to receiving. In recent years, general operating support has constituted only about 15 percent of all grants, with the rest disbursed as project-specific grants. Many institutional funders prefer project grants, in large part because they believe that these grants can be monitored more actively than unrestricted support. One problem with general operating support is that it has come to be associated with "nonessential" items like support staff, rent, and other basic operational expenses that seem extraneous to the core mission. To make matters worse, many funders limit their project support of particular nonprofit organizations to two or three consecutive years. Fearing that they will create a dependence that cannot be sustained indefinitely, traditional institutional funders have settled on a short-term approach to grantmaking that allows them flexibility to change direction quickly should community condition or board interest change. The consequences for nonprofit organizations of this pattern of funding have been predictable: financial instability, programmatic uncertainty, and wasted effort, all of which makes the achievement of real scale and impact difficult.

Venture philanthropy came forward with a different approach to funding, one that offers longer-term support with fewer restrictions. Instead of pulling the plug quickly and moving on to fund other organizations, the venture philanthropy model emphasizes long-term funding commitments designed to help organizations develop and grow. In New York, for example, the Robin Hood Foundation, an early venture philanthropy entrant, has long focused on building lasting relationships with the organizations it supports, with some engagements lasting up to a decade. In a few cases this has translated into large financial commitments, while in other instances the amounts have been modest. By providing large blocks of capacity-building support to nonprofits over longer periods of time, venture philanthropy believes that it will be possible to overcome one of the biggest drawbacks in the nonprofit sector, namely, the inability of nonprofit organizations to achieve real scale and impact.

Before delivering these blocks of support and committing to an organization over the long haul, the venture philanthropists engage in a heavy dose of what they refer to as "due diligence." While it is not entirely clear how this review differs from what all donors have always done (reviewing financial disclosure documents, requiring the presentation of a strategic plan, and submitting to a site visit), the new language is designed to draw attention to the fact that great care needs to be devoted to the decision-making process leading to a commitment. In making the choice of which organizations will be supported, venture philanthropy groups like New Profit Inc. view the ability of a nonprofit organization to achieve scale as a critical consideration. New Profit's long-term investments have focused on organizations like Jumpstart, which is expanding its pre-kindergarten program for disadvantaged children to over a dozen cities around the country.

One of the most visible efforts to apply business know-how to the reform of public schools is being undertaken by John Doerr, a Palo Alto venture capitalist. In 1998 Doerr founded the New Schools Venture Fund (NSVF) with the intention of providing seed capital for promising new for-profit and nonprofit organizations that had the potential to bring movement in the public education field. In choosing organizations to fund, Doerr applies a clear set of criteria. He seeks to support organizations that have strong leadership and that could have a direct impact on school achievement. What made his approach different was he also insisted that the organizations that would receive support had to have a concept that could be brought to scale. Like any business investor, Doerr assembled a team of partners who invested in the fund. In all, some $20 million was raised to fund both nonprofit and for-profit initiatives. NSVF's early nonprofit investments included a comprehensive online guide to California public schools, both nonprofit and for-profit charter school management organizations, a school leadership training program, and a math curriculum development effort. On the for-profit side, NSVF invested in a network of charter schools operated by a for-profit firm. NSVF's approach to school reform continues to reflect a distinctive application of the venture philanthropy model. Drawing on the talents of a group of exceptionally successful entrepreneurs and CEOs, NSVF has developed its own idea about getting to scale: beyond funding organizations that have real potential for growth and impact, NSVF also works to build a network of school reformers through which innovations and ideas can spread. Thus, NSVF both invests and convenes with the aim of maximizing the impact of its investees and moving them to scale.

Beyond delivering larger grants over longer periods of time, venture philanthropy also emphasizes the importance of evaluation or performance management. Funders such as NSVF and New Profit work closely with nonprofits to determine a set of meaningful objectives and a way of tracking progress. The premise of this work is that if a long-term relationship is to be sustained, nonprofits need to be held accountable for their performance. To this end, multidimensional tools for measuring performance have been adapted from the business sector, including the Balanced Scorecard and other attempts to go beyond simple measures of financial performance. There have been efforts to breathe meaning into the concept of "social return on investment," but these have largely collapsed in the face of careful examination. While a few forms of nonprofit activity can be monetized and then subjected to financial analysis, the vast majority of nonprofits engage in work that cannot be converted into simple financial terms. Thus, after some delay and distraction, the venture philanthropy movement settled on more modest efforts to simply calibrate the quality of work and progress toward jointly defined objectives. In carrying out their evaluation work, venture philanthropists seek to encourage nonprofits to manage goals and to be ready to make adjustments in order to improve performance. This focus on measurement bleeds into both the idea of long-term, substantial commitments of funds and the third element of the approach, namely, consultative engagement.

In its effort to reengineer the mainstream model of philanthropy and reorient it toward achieving impact on a broad scale, venture philanthropy has also focused on changing the relationship between the funder and the recipient. Looking at the way many institutional and individual donors carry out their giving, the proponents of venture philanthropy observed that a tremendous amount of effort was being sunk into the process of selecting grant recipients and very little effort was being devoted to helping nonprofit organizations succeed once the check was sent. Indeed, in many foundations, there is today very little follow-up or consultation between the two sides from the time the grant check is mailed to the time the final report on activities is due. One reason that most of the effort of philanthropy is directed at decision making about grants, not effective implementation, is that there is a real pressure on funders to be transparent, fair, and accountable for their actions. Given these demands, it is hardly surprising that many institutional funders have little time for anything other than careful review of applications, site visits before the board meeting, and the writing of recommendations for the board. As grant cycles roll around and around, it can in fact be very hard for funders to break this cycle and engage with recipient organizations in a sustained relationship.

Venture philanthropy takes a different approach to donor/recipient or investor/investee relations, one that extends the time horizon and deepens the contact between all parties. Rather than cut a check and run, venture philanthropy believes that the work only begins once a financial commitment has been made. Given that the commitment is intended to be a long-term one, the new funders have set out to connect directly with the organizations in their portfolios. There are two perceived benefits to a high-engagement strategy. First, nonprofits may learn something that they do not know already, especially if the consulting that is rendered involves specialized skills not usually found in nonprofits. At New Profit Inc., grant recipients receive hands-on assistance from the management consulting giant Monitor Group, which assists with planning growth and tracking progress. For organizations like Citizen Schools, an after-school program that uses adult volunteers to teach teenagers real-world skills through creative projects, this added service is intended to increase the likelihood that the organization will continue to flourish and grow. In lending the expertise of a management consulting firm to their investees, funders are attempting both to protect their investments and increase the social benefits that are achieved.

The second perceived benefit of a consultative and engaged relationship has little to do with nonprofit performance and has everything to do with the satisfaction of the donor. High-engagement philanthropy is a social activity that satisfies the desire of many wealthy people to find meaning in their lives outside of business. Young entrepreneurs who are active in venture philanthropy enjoy taking a hands-on approach and view the process as one of learning and personal growth. At Social Venture Partners (SVP), one of the earliest venture philanthropy efforts, donors commit a minimum of $5,000 to the fund, and in exchange they gain firsthand exposure to the nonprofits that SVP funds. Many of the investors in other venture funds get even more involved in the organizations they fund either by helping with fund-raising or by serving on the board.

There are several assumptions built into the engagement part of the venture philanthropy model. First, that nonprofit organizations want outside help in strategizing and carrying out their work; second, that those offering the consulting have skills that are missing in the nonprofit world and that nonprofits will run better once they have been exposed to these tools and models; and third, that engagement is ethical and appropriate in philanthropy. All three assumptions can reasonably be questioned. One recent survey of the recipients of high-engagement grantmakers found they often complained that the process of working closely with a funder was draining and added little value to their work. As one might expect, the generally tense relationship between benefactor and supplicant is hard to overcome. Many nonprofits believe that the best support is a windowed envelope carrying a no-strings-attached check. Second, when it comes to the skills of high-engagement grantmakers, there is no evidence that the people who control capital in the business sector or those with expertise in for-profit management have any special claim on knowledge about how to create a successful nonprofit organization. Nonprofit mission fulfillment does not always equate to satisfying the demands of clients or responding quickly to market trends. Sometimes, nonprofits need to lead by offering services for which there is little immediate support, but that nevertheless speak to important if overlooked social needs.

Finally, when it comes to the ethics of giving, the central tenets of venture philanthropy appear problematic. Over time, a recurring theme across such faiths as Christianity, Judaism, and Islam is that the donor and the recipient should be separated, so that the recipient is not shamed by having to take money directly from someone else. Anonymous giving promises to ensure that the donor's intent is pure and that the gift is aimed at helping others, rather than gratifying the donor. Venture philanthropy's response to such objections is predictable: venture philanthropists are making investments that are different from charity. Because funds are delivered under different initial terms, the moral problems associated with charity do not apply. Some might even go so far as to say that "social investments" are fundamentally different from grants and that this difference solves any ethical questions that might be posed. Because they are demanding a return when they "invest" their dollars, venture philanthropists feel entitled to actively manage and shape the programs that they support. This is an argument, however, that ultimately rests on semantic hairsplitting and skirts the reality of the asymmetric power in all forms of philanthropy. Besides, there is good reason to believe that the whole idea of turning grants into investments is problematic given the absence of any coherent metrics for measuring return on investment. Still, venture philanthropy's secular, entrepreneurial turn may satisfy the current generation of new entrepreneurial donors eager to express themselves through action in the social sphere.

To date, venture philanthropy remains something of a question mark. To truly make good on the new language created by venture philanthropy, important breakthroughs in practices are needed that create real distance between venture philanthropy and traditional giving. For now, authentic innovations that justify the new terms are difficult to find. Many of the "investments" made by venture philanthropists look just like the "grants" made by other donors. The best evidence of this fact is that many of the organizations supported by venture philanthropists regularly receive grant support from mainline philanthropic funders. In fact, only some of the most high-profile venture philanthropy investments represent substantial portions of the operating budgets of the nonprofit organizations on the receiving end. Similarly, the idea of "consultative engagement" that many describe as a trademark of venture philanthropy is hard to distinguish from the multiple forms of "technical assistance" that donors have provided to nonprofits for decades. Across many of the other terminological divides, the underlying practices do not appear significantly different from what has come before. In one sense, the excitement and energy created by the language of venture philanthropy are positive. New people have been brought into the world of philanthropy and are being converted to the pleasures and challenges of trying to create public value.

At the core, venture philanthropy's search for impact has enlivened the field. After all, the problems of traditional philanthropy are clear and undeniable. There is nevertheless something troubling about the frenzy of verbiage and social venture fund foundings. One thing is impossible to deny, however: by seeking to move concepts and language from the world of business to the world of nonprofit organizations, venture philanthropy must be viewed as a marketing triumph. It has sold a new higher-engagement style of philanthropy to a whole new class of donors. As a set of practical philanthropic innovations, venture philanthropy's contribution to the field remains far harder to ascertain.

Philanthropic Relationships

Venture philanthropy's emphasis on engagement is not without precedent. With the exception of anonymous giving, the world of philanthropy generally does not afford donors the luxury of operating in quiet contemplative isolation. Giving almost always draws the donor and the recipient together into contact as money and missions intercept one another. Yet few relationships are as complex and as highly charged as the one between donor and recipient. Over time, both have settled into a normalized pattern of professional interactions, although important challenges and tensions still exist in this asymmetric relationship. Lurking just beneath the surface are many uncomfortable and unresolved questions about power, class, and race, as well as a fair amount of contempt and suspicion. The sad result is that too many donors and nonprofits interact through a highly stylized form of Kabuki theater built on a ritual of smiles, office chat, and elaborate paperwork. Interviews with nonprofit managers have confirmed that recipient groups have many complaints about their donors. Among the most prominent is the sense of fatigue and bitterness over having to constantly reinvent, recast, and reposition nonprofit activity to please donors and ensure financial survival. As nonprofits try to read donors and give them what they want, fund-raising appeals decrease in their connection to the lived reality of nonprofit organizations and are often thinly veiled attempts to appeal to the interests and needs of the donor. By delivering giving opportunities that will allow donors to pursue projects of interest, at attractive levels of engagement, and with profiles that suit the donors' desires, nonprofits are led to sublimate their real needs and their own preferences for structuring philanthropic relationships. One of the most critical challenges in defining a philanthropic style thus involves taking seriously the distorting effects that a choice can have on the very organizations that donors are trying to help.

Why do the candor and quality of communication between grantmaker and recipient sometimes disintegrate during the funding process? It comes down to two main problems: The *language of needs*—be it for general operating support, capital construction, capacity building, or anything else—has been replaced by a *language of opportunities* designed to appeal to the interests of donors. Appeals for grants have increasingly come to be based more on opportunities for donors, rather than on the needs of recipient organizations, for two reasons. First, financial pressures and competition within the sector are rising quickly. As the sheer number of nonprofit organizations continues to escalate, there is a sense that there will always be a nonprofit organization willing to do whatever it takes to get a grant—even if it means accepting onerous terms. The result is that nonprofits do what they need to do in order to survive. There is also a cultural obstacle to stating needs that stems from the power imbalance in the donor-donee relationship. The guidelines defined by donors appear immutable and definitive to many nonprofits and the easiest response under financial pressure is to craft proposals that present funding opportunities that fit neatly within these parameters.

At the same time, donors have become increasingly proactive in their grantmaking, often telling local nonprofit communities exactly what kinds of proposals they are interested in receiving. The rise of careers in philanthropy and the idea of grantmaking expertise have reinforced this trend toward an increasing role for foundation managers in agenda setting. By encouraging nonprofits to approach funders with requests for capacity-building grants, the venture capital model addresses one important aspect of the nonprofit sector's needs. However, the model ends up circumscribing rather narrowly the type of grants that nonprofits *should* seek. Of course, some nonprofits need assistance in building organizational capacity and infrastructure. Other nonprofits just as surely would benefit from other kinds of support. Ultimately, the focus on project funding and the proactive methods of donors are problematic in many cases, because it shuts down authentic conversations about needs. Rather than directing funding into any single predetermined type of grants, donors and their recipient organizations need to aim for the broader goal of being able to fund a very broad array of grants limited only by the range of authentic needs.

Before embracing the elements of philanthropic style that are part of the venture capital and other business models, donors should first take seriously the possibility that nonprofit managers may well have radically different goals and concerns that need to be both understood, cultivated, and respected—and that these goals may or may not fit within existing definitions of "impact." After all, many nonprofit workers are animated not only by the instrumental goals of service delivery and program performance, but also by a desire to act based on solidarity, commitment to community, and the need to express values through work. Donors need to find a way that nonprofits can safely include these more difficult to document but important goals in their proposals and communications.

Are there donors and nonprofits that have open and honest relations today? Of course. But are there many donors who are not hearing the truth from recipient organizations? Surely. Ultimately, all donors should be able to agree on at least one thing: Any proposal to reengineer philanthropic styles through the application of new business precepts can only be a second step in the process of improving philanthropy. Donors and donees must first work to improve the quality and candor of communication during the process of giving and getting grants. In this sense, one of the key tests for the appropriateness and effectiveness of a philanthropy style is whether it allows the kind of authentic conversation about organizational and community needs that is the basis for sound program planning and development.

How can such a style be crafted? While there is no simple answer to this question, donors must constantly remind themselves of two things. First, nonprofit organizations have a very broad set of needs that may or may not fit within existing foundation guidelines, and no one is served when authentic nonprofit needs are repressed. Second, nonprofits are moved by both instrumental and expressive goals, and while existing performance-based evaluation is important and must continue, other forms of evaluation need to be developed that acknowledge the important although less easily measured nonprofit contributions. Only after honesty is actively cultivated in foundation-nonprofit relations will donors and donees be in a position to act on some of the new models for grantmaking that are now capturing the field's attention. More importantly, getting the relationship between nonprofits and their donors right is critical to the achievement of strategic fit and alignment.

In deciding upon a grantmaking style, one that includes both an engagement level and a preferred profile, donors need to do more than just assess their own private comfort levels. They must ask which form of agency is most aligned with the type of program that is being funded and the structure through which their giving is taking place. Only when the donor's style is understood in terms of its relationship with other points in the philanthropic prism is it possible to come to an assessment of its appropriateness.

Viewing style as contingent and situationally defined is very different from the highly personalized perspective that assumes donors have fixed styles embedded in immutable personality traits, deeply held assumptions, and prior experiences. Instead of seeing the real challenge as one of finding a place in the philanthropic landscape where the donor style finds acceptance, the task becomes one of adjusting and modifying the style depending on the nature of the philanthropic challenge that is to be enjoined. This is not only a strategically attractive approach, but one that eases some of the power asymmetry between giver and recipient. If donors take seriously the idea that their giving style needs to be contextually defined, some of the imbalance in power in philanthropy can be attenuated. This would be a result that not only would satisfy and please nonprofit organizations, but that could also give donors the chance to form more satisfying and balanced relationships with the organizations and causes they support.

CHAPTER FIVE

Time Frames

Timing is an important part of giving. Because philanthropic resources are always limited to some extent, donors have to decide
how much to spend on current needs and how much to conserve for
the future. As a person's wealth and resources increase, the question of timing takes on a special meaning. The trade-offs of current
use compared to future use become starker and the stakes rise substantially. At its core, the timing question in philanthropy involves
a difficult amalgamation of complex conceptual issues, including
a projection into the future of the evolution of a particular problem or issue, an assessment of the benefits of trying to intervene
early, and a consideration of the appropriate discount rate. These
conceptual tasks are complicated by serious limitations related to
the accuracy of any of these projections. However, donors who fail
to engage the timing issue in philanthropy will have a hard time
developing a coherent giving strategy. The timing of giving is in-
extricably connected to the value proposition, the vehicle through
which giving will take place, the style of the donor, and the pursued
theory of change. Thus, all donors must define an appropriate pace
of disbursement, which will vary from a single day to perpetuity.
The payout rate selected will affect both the programmatic impact

donors achieve in the short run and the amount of resources left for future philanthropic efforts in the years ahead.

More often than not, the time dimension within philanthropy is overlooked. Deliberations over the underlying mission or field of activity, explorations of different levels of donor engagement, even the choice of an appropriate vehicle for giving usually attract more attention, interest, and study. Yet the timing through which philanthropic dollars are dispersed is profoundly important because it speaks to the strategic challenge of pacing philanthropy in a way that will fit coherently with the other dimensions of the philanthropic prism. An undefined or ill-defined time horizon for philanthropy can single-handedly undermine a philanthropic strategy.

Although some donors have committed publicly to carrying out all their philanthropy while alive, the majority of large donors opt to spread out their giving over a period of time reaching deep into the future. In making decisions about the timing of their giving, donors must weigh how important their legacy and charitable intent truly are. Over time, experience has taught that it is hard—though not impossible—to maintain control over the governance of philanthropic entities ranging from donor-advised funds in community foundations to private foundations to endowments given to nonprofit organizations such as universities and hospitals. The passing of time has a way of changing the world, the nature of public needs, and the memories and resolve of trustees. Not all donors accept these realities, and many a deceased donor would be appalled to see how time has treated their philanthropic legacy. Still, when donors opt for perpetuity, they are affirming a desire to leave a permanent mark on society that will survive long after their lives are over, an act that is at once a profoundly private expression of the donor's character and values and a strategic choice about how to address public problems. For in choosing a time dimension, donors make a decision both about the speed with which their philanthropic intent will be fulfilled and the pace at which resources will be directed to the fulfillment of public needs.

Social Problems and Time

Just as there is substantial variation in the personal time horizons of donors, so too do public needs have a range of contours over time. The contour of a public need simply refers to the projected evolutionary path of a need or problem over a long period of time, whether the need will increase, diminish, stay the same, or vary unpredictably. The pace of giving over time must be chosen with at least some reference to the contour of the problem being addressed. The fit of the time frame that guides a donor's giving with the projected development of the issue to be addressed is important. In cases in which the costs of delaying action are great—as is the case with major diseases, famines, and intense social crises—donors may need to consider a time frame that privileges current giving. However, when the issue that the donor chooses to address is likely to be present for decades or centuries, as is the case with many global health problems, a longer time frame may well be called for.

At least two other major challenges are associated with thinking about the public purposes addressed by philanthropy over time. First, it is difficult to project far out into the future and know with any certainty how trends will play out. Tremendous uncertainty surrounds social and economic trends, and this uncertainty only increases the further one looks out into the future. While models can help chart trend lines and estimate future needs in a broad range of social areas, the accuracy of these models diminishes as years turn into decades. Moreover, when the social problem is conceptualized broadly (global warming) rather than narrowly (air quality in Denver), more and more uncertainty is inevitably introduced into the equation. Put simply, as the scope of the issue broadens, the amount of noise in the logic model increases, rendering considered judgments into guesses.

The second problem with projecting the shape or contour of a problem is what one might call "the endogeneity problem." It is not clear whether the curves truly represent the shape of a social problem in their ideal and pure form, or whether they really reflect the systemic effects of current and future public and private priorities. In other words, a rising need may reflect inadequacies in the levels of public or private provision that are expected over time rather than current. However, assuming all other intervening factors—including philanthropic expenditures—are stable and do not materially affect the trend line over time is easy if not entirely realistic. Since so little is known in the present about future actions, the trends donors consider come with an important simplifying assumption that all other factors are being held constant and that trends will continue.

Still, a look across the landscape of social problems shows that time affects the evolution of problems dramatically. Take, for example, the case of global environment. If one were to plot over time the trend line for environmental problems, it would look like a relatively steep ascending curve, at least as measured by greenhouse gases, air and water quality, and other global indicators of environmental stress. The data is such that any informed donor would rightly conclude that action now and in the future is likely to be needed. Yet in making a decision about when to give, now or far off in the future, the donor must make a difficult judgment about the probability that his charitable intervention is likely to significantly change the steepness of the curve. If it will not and if philanthropy is by a simple order of magnitude irrelevant to the future contour of the problem, then there may be a good reason to conserve resources and save them for when they will be needed even more urgently. Yet there is something troubling in this sort of analysis. If donors with limited resources can have no effect on the future shape of a social problem, then one might well ask why give at all. Of course, the answer lies in the way the breadth of a social problem is defined. One donor might reasonably seek to take on the issue of urban sprawl around Chicago, while another pushes for international agreements on CO_2 emissions. In this sense, strategic giving starts with and demands not only thought about the timing of giving but also in the boundaries around the problem to be addressed. Only

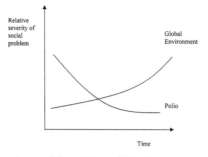

Fig. 5.1: Projected evolution of the problems of global environment and polio over time.

when donors choose areas in which their giving is likely to have an effect on the future course of events can they truly claim to be doing anything remotely strategic.

Consider next the reverse situation. If environmental problems are getting more serious, there are many areas where the severity of the problem is diminishing. Since the development of the polio vaccine, the scale and human toll wrought by this disease has been shrinking (see fig. 5.1). Over time, the number of children victimized by polio has dropped precipitously in developed countries and has been reduced significantly in developing countries. The Bill and Melinda Gates Foundation today is spending hundreds of millions of dollars on vaccinations in those parts of the world where the disease is still present. It is useful to consider the issue of endogeneity in this work. In the case of polio, while the trend is in the right direction, donors remain active in this field precisely because they believe there is a link between the future shape of the problem and the level of current philanthropic activity. That is, giving today will allow the problem to recede faster than if nothing were done. On the surface, social problems exhibiting a downward-sloping curve appear to be low-leverage opportunities, in that, even in the absence of giving, the problem will likely diminish. In reality, such situations do offer opportunities, especially when even small increments of change are meaningful due to the high stakes.

Some public needs are more complex and variable. Take, for example, the case of AIDS in the United States. As the disease spread in the 1980s at high rates, the need for interventions was acute. Today the rate of infection is lower and the range of treatments is far greater. The curve for AIDS in the United States thus exhibits a convex shape (see fig. 5.2). For donors, this raises an interesting issue in terms of the timing of their giving: If active public and private funding of research and public information efforts in the 1990s helped turn the curve downward, are future philanthropic efforts in this area likely to be as valuable as ones made in the short term? The answer lies in where along this line one situates the present. If one believes that we are somewhere just past the apex of the curve, then more giving in the short run will likely help to drive the curve downward in a significant way. If, however, one believes that we are well past the apex and already into the decline, giving in the present or in the future may be harder to justify, especially if other causes are calling. Here, the endogeneity problem is severe. To be sure, some problems come and go as demographic shifts work themselves out, but in most cases bending the curve is likely to be the product of intervention and investment. Thus, in the case of polio, the bend would have been unlikely in the absence of substantial public and private investment in research and public information. The best evidence of this endogeneity is the course the disease has taken overseas, where efforts to combat the disease started later and were far weaker than in developed nations.

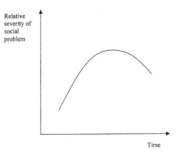

Fig. 5.2: Projected evolution of the problem of AIDS in the United States over time.

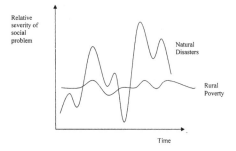

Fig. 5.3: Projected evolution of the problems of natural disasters and rural poverty over time.

Of course, some problems remain relatively constant in terms of their intensity over time. In the case of rural poverty, the rates have varied little over the past five decades, even with the introduction of many publicly funded initiatives aimed at helping the rural poor (see fig. 5.3). Variations in the poverty rate for this group have proven to be closely related to the state of the national economy, with recessions imposing a fair amount of pain on the most vulnerable workers. For donors interested in combating poverty, the presence of a relatively flat line is once again conceptually challenging in terms of defining a time frame for giving. One strategy might be to acknowledge that the issue is driven heavily by macroeconomic trends and that the role of philanthropy may simply be to respond consistently over time to need. Under such a strategy, conserving funds and limiting current expenditures so as to be able to respond over the long run would be one plausible course of action. Another approach might be to seek to minimize the social stress by undertaking broader, more integrated steps to move people out of poverty. By acting aggressively in the short run, donors might be able to tilt the trend line downward. Again, the timing of giving depends heavily on other factors.

An additional scenario is possible. There are some social needs that become extremely acute for short periods of time, then recede, only to reemerge later. The most obvious example is disaster relief.

Organizations such as the American Red Cross are constantly going through periods of heavy activity aimed at helping devastated communities following hurricanes, fires, and floods. While there is a general ability to predict the timing of this work based on years of experience, it is impossible to know with any real certainty when these periods will occur and how closely grouped together the events will be. This can make planning charitable activity extremely difficult and requires a capacity to mobilize to render assistance well before the financial support for the particular intervention has been secured. For disaster relief, a short response time is required. While some donors deliberate for weeks, months, or years before beginning a charitable initiative, any donor seeking to work in a field as unpredictable and chaotic as disaster relief must be willing to make decisions quickly and decisively.

In considering the shape of the problem that a donor will tackle, clear geographical boundaries are important. Depending on the breadth or narrowness of these boundaries—local, regional, national, international—the timing of philanthropic strategies will vary considerably. As the focus broadens, the time horizon, to some extent, must extend outward. Dealing with youth violence on the South Side of Chicago, let alone the whole city, is a formidable task. Dealing with the issue nationally is another matter altogether. And trying to work on youth violence on an international scale is an entirely different proposition. As a donor's focus broadens, two things must happen: first, the amount of money devoted to a problem must be increased and, second, the time allocated for action must be extended.

The time horizon of a donor will be conditioned by the way boundaries are drawn around the problem the donor chooses to address. A realistic assessment of the temporal contour of the problem and its relationship to the chosen pace of disbursement is central to effective philanthropy. The issue of how quickly or how slowly a donor spends his philanthropic capital is often referred to as the payout rate. It is a subject that is at the center of the regulation and oversight of private foundations, but since the payout rate determines the speed of giving, the concept has not only legal but strategic importance.

The Payout Rate Decision

The time dimension of philanthropy is translated most often into the operational question of setting a payout rate or the percent of assets to be devoted each year to charitable purposes. For individual donors, the payout question can be a simple function of the willingness of donors to part with funds sooner or later, and the resulting speed with which their giving unfolds. For private foundations, the payout rate is the rate of expenditure from the endowment, which is mandated by law to be a minimum of 5 percent of the monthly average value of the endowment over the previous year. In thinking about the rate in which philanthropic funds are spent, there are at least three significant issues at play: effectiveness, equity, and values expression.

EFFECTIVENESS

The oldest argument for faster rates of philanthropic disbursals harkens back to scientific philanthropy's early claims over Victorian charity and is grounded in beliefs about effectiveness. Giving away larger amounts of money today rather than off in the future is attractive because it could make it easier for donors to actually solve social problems within communities, rather than merely treat the symptoms of social disorder. To be effective, donors need to perform preventive giving. By getting to the root causes and by committing large blocks of philanthropic capital in the short run, donors can in principle avoid having to spend larger amounts of money over longer periods of time. In some fields, such as medical research, funding work today has considerably more value than funding research twenty, fifty, or even a hundred years from now. In cases like this, in which problems are likely to grow in the absence of philanthropic interventions, acting aggressively in the present may be more efficient.

Of course, this whole line of argument rests on the assumption that philanthropic interventions are likely to be able to get to the root causes of such problems as poverty and not just relieve the visible symptoms (e.g., unemployment) by offering short-term programs (e.g., job training). For this assumption to be plausible, donors would need to commit not only large amounts of funds in the present, but over time continue to devote resources to the real pursuit of the underlying causes of such problems as poverty. Unfortunately, there is little evidence that even if donors could spend funds in a concentrated and focused way on targeting root causes, they would be able to solve problems that in many cases have persisted for centuries. Moreover, a good case can be made that particular social problems may become more acute than they are today—regardless of how much short-term effort is devoted to addressing the problem. For the fatalistic donor, it is hard to see many problems becoming smaller and less daunting in the future. In fact, some donors might reasonably argue that many areas are likely to grow substantially in their urgency over time, and that conservative spending of charitable funds today is needed to ensure that large amounts of philanthropic dollars are available to address these problems in the future when they become even more pronounced.

There is at least one other dimension to the effectiveness claim about spending more in the present in an attempt to reach the root causes of problems. If donors were to push large amounts of money out into the nonprofit sector, rather than place it in perpetual endowments, it is unclear whether nonprofit organizations could absorb and use effectively substantially larger amounts of money in a short period of time. The payout question in philanthropy involves not only the interests and needs of donors. It has clear practical implications for the broader nonprofit sector, which uses charitable funds to deliver services. For some donors thinking about the question of achieving their philanthropic purposes, substantially increasing the flow of grants to nonprofits is not an obviously efficient way to increase social impact—especially if smaller, local, and less sophisticated nonprofits lack the infrastructure to direct these additional funds to productive uses. Moreover, there is always the question of whether growth and scale are universally desirable ends, with many believing that nonprofit agencies are most effective when they are small and tightly linked to local communities. In some areas of activity, there may well be diminishing returns on philanthropic investments. In the area of public policy advocacy, for example, funding new research and public information in those fields already saturated by well-funded groups may not be particularly effective. Nor would it be particularly promising to seek to turn a small community service organization into a national nonprofit through one sudden large infusion of cash. In some cases, funds need to be provided at a pace that matches the capacity of nonprofits to grow and use the funds most effectively.

EQUITY

An alternative argument for current use over future use is more subtle and touches on equity concerns. The whole question of philanthropic payouts has serious fairness implications, especially given the exponential growth in the size of philanthropic assets expected in the coming decades. For some, a higher payout rate may make sense if intergeneration equity is a concern. To be sure, money earned in one generation does not entail a moral or legal obligation to help those who either contributed to one's success or who did not fare as well. Some donors are nevertheless interested in returning some of their wealth in the form of helping others. For this group, the idea of deferring giving until old age, or even further off in the future through the establishment of a foundation, is unappealing. It would create an intergenerational gap that would make it hard for the donor to recognize and thank others. Thus, for individual donors, the temporal dimension of giving raises the difficult question of just who is entitled to receive the public benefits that philanthropy can create. Some donors answer this question by giving out their funds faster and sooner so as to concentrate the effect of those most proximate circumstances surrounding the creation of the wealth.

The equity issue is somewhat different for private foundations, most of which are established in perpetuity. Foundations have long represented one of the few alternatives to paying high estate taxes, which for many years surpassed 50 percent on large estates. When a foundation is created today, the burden of lost tax revenue is borne by citizens now in the form of a tax expenditure. However, the benefits of any particular foundation's giving largely do not accrue to the citizens who made the tax expenditure that allowed its establishment. Research has shown that the vast majority of private foundations give out each year close to the minimum defined by law, namely, 5 percent of the value of their assets. By giving the wealthy the opportunity to create foundations in perpetuity, taxpayers today are in essence being asked to subsidize the welfare of future generations, at a time when many current social needs continue to be unmet. This ever-evolving intergenerational transfer of resources would be unproblematic if each generation made tax expenditures of roughly equal size. This is likely not the case, however. As demographic waves of different sizes and with different levels of resources age and convey their wealth into foundations, the unequal intergenerational distribution of foundation assets will become pronounced. Just as the burdens and benefits of Social Security are not distributed equally across generations, so too will low foundation payouts in perpetuity create intergenerational inequities. Higher payout rates down the road may be needed to even out the costs and benefits of foundation giving.

VALUES EXPRESSION

The third rationale for prioritizing current needs and current giving stems from the fact that spending today rather than saving for tomorrow has the benefit of allowing the donor to take part in and enjoy the act of giving. Bob Buford, a major donor in Texas interested in assisting churches and faith-based charitable work, has declared that he intends to do all his giving himself so that he can enjoy translating the fruits of his business success into actions helping causes that are important to him. While this is an extreme position, many donors have begun to do more of their giving while alive simply because they want to enjoy their giving and see their interests and aspirations fulfilled while they are still here. For such donors, giving today oneself makes more sense than giving in the future by someone else.

This may ultimately be the most compelling argument for paying out funds sooner rather than later. Given the tremendous uncertainty over whether greater levels of impact will be achieved by attempting to root out problems in the short run, and given the unclear question about intergenerational inequities of foundations, there is little doubt that calling on donors to spend their funds faster, during their lives, rather than slower creates at least one clear benefit for all: it ensures that philanthropy is animated by the kinds of passions and convictions that only individuals hold. From the perspective of the public interest, having philanthropic principals, not their agents, carry out philanthropy should be a priority since this is the best way to ensure that philanthropy's unique voice in the public sphere continues to be heard loudly and that it speaks in ways that are different and less constrained than the government.

Yet there is and will always be resistance to this argument. Centering principally on the question of particularism and elite control, having donors do their own giving while alive will appear to involve a large unproven assumption that this kind of giving will, in the long run, prove more beneficial for society than giving that is moderated by disinterested agents working within the regulated confines of a foundation or other institutional context. The flaw in this counterclaim is simply that it misses the point that philanthropy is not only about the efficient satisfaction of public needs, but also involves the satisfaction of the donors in seeing their wealth transformed from private property into something bigger and broader, namely, the intersection of their values with some community or public purpose. The timing or payout question in philanthropy thus cannot be understood strictly on the basis of how it affects the public in terms of net benefits realized. It must also be understood as having a significant component that is focused on the expressive character of philanthropy, which allows it to contribute to pluralism. Alongside the arguments related to effectiveness and equity, the timing of philanthropic giving ultimately bring the discussion right back to the fundamental question of what truly is the underlying purpose of philanthropy. I suggested earlier that while there are many answers to this question, the affirmation of pluralism through expressive acts of caring may be different and more universal than the other more narrowly instrumental functions of philanthropy.

The Idea of Discounting

If the question of how much to give today and how much to give tomorrow appears complex, it gets even more challenging as soon as one begins to unpack the analytical issues it raises. A central issue is that of philanthropic discounting, or how the value of giving is measured over time. In theory, discounting could be a useful analytic frame for donors who are planning to pay out philanthropic funds over time, a frame that points to how a sustained consideration of time must inform decisions about giving. If it could be applied to philanthropy, discounting would allow a donor to consider how much future giving will cost in today's dollars. Such information could inform the timing of gifts and the pace at which funds are disbursed. The case for some kind of discounting in philanthropy is straightforward enough: discounting recognizes that all asset allocation decisions have opportunity costs. To make informed decisions, be they financial or philanthropic, alternatives need to be known and understood. Donors, formally or informally, routinely evaluate competing grant requests to determine the "best" possible allocation of the limited pool of grant money available. The practice of discounting extends the notion of opportunity costs to broader decisions over time in a systematic and rigorous manner.

The idea of discounting is roughly analogous to the more familiar idea of compounding. While compounding tells us what investment funds will be worth in the future given a set of assumptions about rates of return, discounting tells us what grant funds at some point in the future are worth today, based on similar assumptions. Discounting captures the importance of time in shaping the choices we face about how to use limited resources. When applied in the world of business and government, it is a means to confront methodically difficult questions about inter-temporal choices that are wrapped up in many significant decisions. As donors contemplate how to use philanthropic resources over time, discounting could be a tool that would remind them that the competing claims of future generations need to be weighed against those of the current generation. If it could be adapted meaningfully to philanthropy, discounting would allow donors to plan the timing of their philanthropy systematically. However, complications present themselves quickly.

One critical consideration when weighing the value of a future philanthropic dollar against a current philanthropic dollar is the selection of an appropriate discount rate. Discounting is really just a concept until it is rendered operational through the specification of a discount rate. The higher the discount rate, the greater the opportunity cost is of spending today rather than in the future. Conversely, when the discount rate is low, future philanthropic giving appears to cost closer to the same as giving today. Since philanthropy prides itself on tackling difficult social problems that require sustained intervention and support, donors often must work methodically on complex social problems over long periods of time. As they do so, donors might be wise to place their philanthropic decisions in a framework that includes some notion that time matters in philanthropy. The problem in philanthropy is that it is very hard in practice to come up with a clear and compelling case for a given discount rate. Holding all else constant, donors might be tempted to begin their search for a philanthropic discount rate by looking to the rate that they would earn from their financial investments. Why would the rate of return on financial investments be relevant to a philanthropic discount rate? The answer lies in the fact that the financial rate of return earned by an endowment indicates what sensibly invested funds not donated today will be worth in the future. In the context of a foundation with an endowment to be managed, any funds not given away today will instead be invested in a financial account where they will earn the financial rate of return. The opportunity cost of making the grant today rather than the following year thus begins to look like the foregone return that the retained funds would have earned. But there are problems with this approach.

Since the expected rate of return varies dramatically depending on how much risk one is willing to assume in investing an endowment, it should come as no surprise that the discount rate would have to be different for different donors. Some donors have a higher tolerance for risk in pursuit of higher rates of return, while others have a low tolerance for risk. To peg the lower bound of the discount rate, one that has almost no risk and thus provides a very conservative estimate of the value of the future dollar, one might look to the interest rate on long-term U.S. government bonds. Given the fact that most donors are willing to assume some risk in their investments, the actual discount rate would more likely be calculated by taking a weighted average of the expected return from stocks and bonds. But the rate of financial return, while providing a tempting benchmark for setting a philanthropic discount rate, turns out to be an inadequate point of reference.

This basic philanthropic decision about the comparative value of giving now or later is complicated by at least three factors that would not be taken into consideration if the simple financial discount rate were applied. First, donors do not know the extent to which the social problems on which they choose to focus will become exacerbated or attenuated as a result of forgoing acting immediately. In order to discount accurately, it would be necessary to have a firm understanding of how bad conditions are likely to be in the future. This is difficult to know, and often projections about social problems have proven to be far off the mark. Second, donors do not know how the cost of administering and implementing non-profit services will evolve over the years. Some fields will have high rates of cost escalation while others will be much flatter. Without being able to know for sure the nonprofit inflation rate in particular fields, it would be very difficult to know what costs will be in the future in order to accurately discount them. Third, donors may be working on multiple issues over time, and each will have its own discount rate. Few donors devote all their resources to one particular issue or purpose over a length of time. In practice, many of the larger institutional donors have tremendous freedom to change and adapt over the years, as social problems arise. In addition, many of these funders are operating simultaneously in multiple fields. To discount accurately, careful calculation across each field would be needed.

Like all actors facing a difficult inter-temporal decision, donors are likely to be tempted to rely on reasonable simplifying assumptions: namely that social problems will evolve as they have over time, that program costs will rise modestly like everything else, and that differences across fields will even out in the long run. We know, for example, that many of the most pressing social problems are rarely subject to sudden reversal or dramatic decline. While there is no "donor price index" that can easily be consulted, the costs of delivering services in the nonprofit sector have not evolved demonstrably differently from those in the broader economy. Across fields, we know that all nonprofits face rising costs to some degree and that the difference between higher education, a notorious outlier in the sector, and other nonprofits may not reflect the broader sector's more moderated trends. On the whole, the past gives donors a reasonable point of departure for thinking about how the context for philanthropy will evolve over the years. Only by making reasonable simplifying assumptions can donors begin to see and adjust to the undeniable fact that philanthropic funds spent in the present need to be valued differently than funds spent some time in the distant future.

This much said, there are still some large obstacles to rendering the idea of philanthropic discounting applicable to the world of giving. Chief among them is translating a mathematical calculation into a strategic planning process. A first step might be to note that donors engage in some kind of calculus about social benefits each and every time they award a grant to one qualified applicant while denying a grant to another qualified applicant. In deciding what programs to support, donors routinely make judgments about the comparative value of different grantmaking options based on the social benefits that are likely to accrue. This is an imprecise science, but one that is needed when trying to sort out the many competing substantive claims on philanthropic resources. On the other hand, in deciding how much to give now versus in the future, it is more appropriate for donors to think in terms of the costs of competing inter-temporal strategies. The discounting approach described therefore draws attention to the costs of the various alternative strategies available to donors, while bracketing some of the measurement problems associated with the assessment of the benefits of specific grantmaking decisions. If some of the obstacles could be overcome or at least rendered manageable, discounting would make it possible to compare the cost of acting immediately versus waiting to make a grant, and, in the process, allow one to attack some critical issues in grantmaking strategy.

Interestingly, the two most common criticisms of discounting—particularly prominent in the field of environmental policy—have traditionally been ethical in character and do not relate to the difficulty in setting a rate or implementing this mode of thinking. The first is that discounting unfairly privileges the present generation at a cost to future generations. In the area of philanthropy, some might reasonably argue that equating the philanthropic discount rate with the financial rate of return would lead to an unacceptably low valuation of future philanthropic benefits. This objection misses the point that discounting simply applies the logic of compounding and helps us recognize that funds not spent now but that are invested will grow over time, which will make greater resources available for future generations. Discounting reflects this fact, makes no ethical judgment about who is more or less deserving, and thus puts all generations on equal footing.

Critics of discounting might offer a second objection by asking how donors can reasonably apply a test to their giving that says that a life saved in the future is worth less than a life saved today. Since philanthropy often attacks difficult problems facing the most needy and vulnerable members of society, discounting might appear to cheapen philanthropy and subject its opportunity costs to a primitive comparison to the return on financial assets. The practice of discounting would thus seem like a questionable, if not untenable, proposition. The difficulty of sustaining this moral position is that it simply does not answer the question posed by philanthropic discounters. In essence, the donor who refuses to discount on moral grounds substitutes a normative question (What do we owe future generations?) each time the foundation that discounts poses an analytic question (How do we balance the donor needs of future generations with those of the current one?). These two questions are different enough to make one realize that defining a core problem in philanthropy as one of addressing issues of efficiency and intergenerational equity quickly pushes giving into the competing realms of analytics and ethics.

The conflicting analytic and ethical questions raised by foundation giving also demonstrate that thoughtful philanthropy involves confronting both obligations and opportunity costs. Philanthropic discounting is a first step toward finding a solution to the deeper and more politically charged questions of deciding how much donors should pay out in grants now versus how much they should pay out in the future, a decision that has multibillion-dollar implications. Discounting—even if only used as a tool for defining strategy and framing central questions and concerns—can be an important focusing device for donors who pay out philanthropic funds over time, a device that draws their attention to the complex time dimension in philanthropy.

Donors' Definition of the Time Dimension

Outside the world of private foundations, a growing number of individual donors have begun to seek answers to the question of when to do their giving. Some have taken bold and decisive steps to confront the issue of intergenerational equity, witness the rise of "mega-gifts," which in several cases have reached into the hundreds of millions of dollars. Many members of the new generation of major donors, drawn increasingly from the ranks of successful business entrepreneurs, have declared their commitment to doing their own giving during their own lifetimes. The rise of these "do-it-yourself" donors along with the appearance of new, more flexible vehicles for philanthropy for smaller donors (such as the charitable gift funds now offered by mutual fund companies) have helped open new channels outside of foundation philanthropy for exploring the meaning of the responsibilities of wealth. This choice between giving while alive or after death is a personal one that depends on whether donors feel a calling for philanthropy or whether they believe they can best contribute to society by building wealth and leaving the giving to others.

Some very wealthy individuals have postponed their philanthropy precisely because they believe their greatest social contribution is building wealth that others can then disburse at a later time. Entrepreneur John D. MacArthur, who made a fortune in the insurance and real estate fields but left most of his wealth to others to give away, famously declared: "I figured out how to make the money. You fellows [at the MacArthur Foundation] will have to figure out how to spend it." In other cases, smaller donors have made the news only upon their death when it is revealed that they focused on saving their money during their lives so that others could later benefit. In these and many other cases, it is apparent that philanthropy beckons people in different ways.

When wealthy people eschew giving during their lives, they may have a host of reasons that have little to do with a rational calculus of a discount rate. Instead, it simply may reflect an unwillingness to confront their own mortality or the inability to make a decision about what causes are worth supporting. By linking the donor's name to philanthropic institutions that are established in perpetuity, philanthropy can allow the donor to live—or at least have his or her legacy live—forever. However, the idea of perpetuity is not a simple and uncomplicated one. After all, there is something at once very noble and presumptuous about the idea of philanthropic legacies living on forever and good deeds being done in the name of someone long since gone. Presumptuous, in that forever is a very, very long time. Noble, in that the impulse to establish a foundation in perpetuity represents a selfless and caring act to project good work across time to unknown legions of persons. It means that donors are able to project the benefits of their giving way off into the future and in the process separate themselves from the act of giving. Perpetuity also means that the donor is willing to trust others to act in keeping with a more or less clearly defined charitable intent and to do so in a way to benefit people who are not yet even born.

The Challenge of Time

For donors confronting the challenge of devising a strategy for giving, the time dimension may not appear at first blush to be a pressing issue. After all, questions relating to purpose and institutional structure seem more urgent and technically challenging. To avoid thinking about the time dimension in philanthropy would be a serious mistake, however. For timing affects not just the rate at which funds are expended, but the way giving is organized, the identity and engagement of the donor, the use or avoidance of institutional arrangements, and even the very choice of fundamental purposes to be pursued. Meeting the challenge of time in philanthropy requires that donors think carefully about both the time horizon of the public problem they are interested in addressing and the significance and permanence they attach to their own charitable intent.

The time dimension to giving demands not only thought about the timing of a donation, but also the timing of the use of the gift. Donors need to make a judgment about when and at what pace their philanthropic resources should be consumed by recipient organizations. Some donors, particularly those who support universities, prefer to make endowment gifts that offer the promise of permanence. There is of course a high price for the stability that endowment funding offers: it often requires a commitment of more than twenty times the amount that is to be spent on an annual basis. This means that large philanthropic resources need to be transferred from the control of the donor to the recipient organization in order to gain the benefits of perpetuity. The rate at which funds are transferred from donor to recipient reflects to some extent the degree of trust between the two parties. With the exception of large institutions such as universities, hospitals, and museums, endowment funding is typically given only after an organization has proven itself through the wise use of annual operating support. Finding the right pace at which to transfer philanthropic resources will also be significantly shaped by the level of engagement the donor has with the recipient organization. With greater levels of personal contact with senior leaders in nonprofits and with full familiarity with programmatic content, donors will feel more at ease transferring funds sooner rather than later and in larger rather than smaller installments.

Construing the time dimension of giving properly becomes progressively more difficult as the underlying value to be produced through giving becomes more complex and multidimensional. For donors who have single-interest agendas, thinking about the right pace at which to disburse funds, varying somewhere between giving everything away immediately to giving slowly indefinitely, will be a reasonably manageable task. It will involve some primitive attempts to think about how to adjust the future value of interventions against the present value of giving, taking into consideration a range of factors that impinge on how much discount should be applied. For donors with complex missions and with program operations spread across a range of subject fields, the discounting exercise will be less fruitful given the sheer complexity of the streams of expenditures and benefits that would need to be assessed. Still, even though discounting should be understood more as a heuristic device than as an actual operational tool, the time dimension of giving needs to be taken into consideration as a plan for giving is shaped.

These complications aside, the philanthropic challenge remains unambiguously clear: to fashion a giving strategy that takes into consideration the temporal dimension of giving and the inextricable link of time to the other elements of the philanthropic prism. Having witnessed the phenomenal growth rate of the foundation field over the past decades, many donors start with the assumption that their giving will go on forever and that the right institutional arrangement for them is thus a foundation. There are, I have suggested, good reasons, from both the perspective of the donor and of the public, to resist this impulse. The time dimension of giving can be the starting point for the construction of a philanthropic giving plan, but because time limits the options across the other dimensions of the philanthropic prism, it may be in the best interests of donors and the public to resist this temptation. Choosing between current giving and the slow disbursal of funds in perpetuity is ultimately a personal choice for donors that has profound implications for the organizations and individuals that stand to benefit from the giving. One thing is certain: treating time as something complex and contingent—and not just simply accepting the default position of perpetuity—is critical to philanthropy moving toward greater levels of strategic alignment and coherence.

CHAPTER SIX

Institutions and Vehicles

Giving can no longer be conceived only as an act linking isolated individuals to social causes. Today important parts of philanthropy are transacted through philanthropic institutions and vehicles that stand between the donor and the recipient and through which philanthropic funds are delivered. Over time, the organizational landscape of philanthropy has grown increasingly more crowded, as more and more organizational forms have come to populate the terrain. The decision to conduct one's giving in part or completely through an institution, and the choice of the appropriate institution, must be guided by a careful consideration of all the dimensions in the philanthropic prism. The choice of the right institutional vehicle for giving is an element of strategy building that demands constant and careful consideration to ensure that the features of the vehicle and the goals of the donor are in fact aligned. Few decisions in philanthropy can quickly either make giving more satisfying or turn it into a painful exercise.

Beyond the obvious choice of a private foundation established in perpetuity, donors have an ever-expanding range of options. They can contribute to a community foundation, an operating foundation, or, if their wealth is tied up in a business, a company-sponsored

129

foundation. For smaller donors, federations such as the United Way beckon, as do new vehicles such as gift funds and giving circles that promise alternatively great administrative efficiency or peer counsel through collaboration. These options are supplemented by a range of more complex choices involving various forms of trusts. According to tax lawyers, sorting out these options involves a complex calculation focused on tax savings and estate-planning issues. In reality, the decision about the vehicle to be used, if one is to be used at all, involves a whole group of considerations that have little to do with finances. An appropriate philanthropic vehicle, though, will enable donors to accomplish their giving better.

If one accepts the premise that philanthropy involves more than just the instrumental pursuit of public benefits as it also includes the expression and fulfillment of the donor's values and commitments, then the choice of institutions needs to be judged by how well it supports both these dimensions of philanthropy. In order to improve the benefits of giving and to maximize the personal satisfaction that giving can bring to the donor, it is important for donors to make an informed decision about the institutional form to be used. By exploring here some of the trade-offs and opportunities that donors face in the choice of philanthropic vehicles, it may be possible to begin to identify how and why institutional forms coincide—and at times conflict—with the process of attempting to move toward strategic giving.

Four Classic Forms of Foundations

In common parlance, a "foundation" has become shorthand for a private or independent foundation, which makes grants to nonprofit organizations using earnings of its endowment. Constituted by a board and sometimes a staff, a foundation reviews grant applications and disburses funds to those applicants deemed most deserving. Three other types of foundations do not fit this image, however. Operating foundations use endowment interest to fund program activities carried out by foundation staff, community foundations solicit endowment funds from residents of the surrounding city or region, and corporate foundations owe their existence to annual contributions from a share of corporate profits or a percentage of an endowment, if one exists. These three new philanthropic vehicles are all based on the model of the private foundation, although each has its own distinctive organizational structure and practices. All four organizational forms of philanthropy have established themselves and gained currency because each represents a different strategic response to a combination of external pressures and internal management.

OPERATING FOUNDATIONS

Operating foundations are endowed philanthropic institutions that use investment income to operate programs run by the foundation's own staff rather than to make grants to outside organizations. Operating foundations have both endowments and substantive programs and thus have characteristics of both conventional foundations and more generic grant-seeking nonprofit organizations. In understanding the hybrid structure of operating foundations, the concept of transaction costs turns out to be useful. In attempting to give an account of why giant firms have emerged and replaced smaller, more specialized firms, economists claim that this move represents the most efficient way to produce goods for an industrial society. In transaction costs analysis, all organizations are understood as sets of contracts that collectively determine governance structure. In managing their affairs and complex web of agreements, firms seek to minimize transaction costs to gain a competitive advantage. This can be done in two basic ways. First, firms can work through the external market and seek out the best possible deals. Second, they can operate through internal hierarchy and control the production process from start to finish.

Economists argue that a key determinant of how organizations solve their problem of obtaining needed resources is the relative specificity of the asset. When a particular physical or human asset becomes specialized and difficult to obtain in the market, firms will attempt to secure the asset through ownership rather than through spot contracting. The need to minimize transaction costs, manage uncertainty, and secure assets leads firms to buy out suppliers or subcontractors. This leads to a small number of larger firms organized as hierarchies, rather than a large number of small firms contracting with one another in the market.

These transaction costs concepts are pertinent to the institutional landscape and allow one to understand the appearance of operating foundations: they are able to fulfill their missions most efficiently through internal hierarchy because of the high transaction costs associated with working through the external grants marketplace. Both the structure and practices of operating foundations can thus be usefully understood from the perspective of transaction costs economics.

An example may prove helpful. The Liberty Fund in Indianapolis, Indiana, is an operating foundation with a large endowment that uses its resources to promote libertarian principles through a range of publications and conferences. The Liberty Fund uses its philanthropic resources to produce and distribute at a subsidized price copies of the works of political writers with a commitment to liberty. The fund also publishes a series of volumes that offers to students, scholars, and the general public handsome editions of all the work of Adam Smith at low prices. The interest generated by the endowment is also used to host a series of conferences around the country each year where works in the classical liberal tradition are discussed. These conferences are held at resorts from coast to coast, and participants have all their expenses paid by the fund. Rather than contract out all of the work of organizing these meetings, the fund has a number of full-time support staff who work on hotel and travel arrangements for participants. In addition, the fund's professional staff travels to each of the seminars and helps organize the meetings and guide discussions of the selected texts. Editors and conference leaders are employees of the fund rather than a recipient organization, which allows the Liberty Fund a great deal of control over its program, something that is not usually possible in a grantmaking relationship.

If operating foundations represent an efficient response to a changing philanthropic landscape, the following question naturally arises: why haven't all grantmaking foundations turned into operating foundations? The answer lies in the tremendous variety of charitable missions that exist in American philanthropy. For large foundations pursuing broad social agendas, such as improving the education of children or providing job training for the unemployed, working through a hierarchy is often impossible or impractical. For such philanthropic organizations, grantmaking is the only alternative. Not only does grantmaking allow foundations to pool resources through jointly funded projects, but it also gives foundations the ability to move quickly in responding to changing social needs. Only when the mission is more narrow and related to research does the structure of an operating foundation become more attractive.

Operating foundations are frequently viewed as aberrations on the philanthropic scene, strangers who have abdicated the traditional arm's-length relationship between grantmaker and grant recipient. Operating foundations are, however, better viewed as efficiency maximizers that fulfill their philanthropic missions through hierarchy, rather than in the traditional grant market. In this way, the emergence of operating foundations can be interpreted as a response to the rising costs of grantmaking: operating foundations represent an organizational form within philanthropy that permits a high level of control, low transaction costs, and—in certain program areas—increased efficiency. For some donors and for some missions, operating foundations are an institutional option that can help achieve a high level of strategic fit and alignment.

COMMUNITY FOUNDATIONS

Community foundations are philanthropic institutions set up in cities or regions, which allow residents to make contributions and give their estates to one large foundation. Unlike most private foundations, community foundations depend on a steady stream of inputs or contributions to grow their corpus. Interestingly, community foundations have experienced a period of phenomenal growth over the past few decades, with hundreds of new institutions sprouting up in small and midsize cities around the country. One of the reasons for the popularity of community foundations is that they are easy to start. All that is needed is an initial gift. In this way, continual dependency on donors is a central feature of community foundations, one that is not present in private, independent foundations.

The dependence of community foundations on outside donors for philanthropic resources makes the foundations accountable for their philanthropic decisions. Community residents can review past grants, talk to foundation staff, and work out arrangements that meet their philanthropic interests—all before committing their funds to a community foundation. Community foundations in this sense are more "public" than independent or private foundations, whose grantmaking is not shaped by a need to attract resources. Community foundations' dependence on outside resources invariably breeds broad grantmaking programs, as community foundations become large department stores where donors can find the philanthropic wares they are seeking.

The defining features of community foundations can be usefully understood from a resource-dependency perspective. Resource dependence argues that organizations are defined by their need to secure and distribute resources. Organizations are not self-sufficient because they almost never possess all the resources needed to survive. Most organizations depend on resources from the outside and must establish structures and implement strategies aimed at ensuring that the flow of goods and services coming in and leaving their organization remains open. The resource-dependence model stresses the role played by interdependence as a mechanism for adaptation to changing conditions in the environment around the organization. According to the resource-dependence model, organizational structure and development can be understood by looking at the environment within which the organization operates. The complex patterns of resource flows—and the relative degree of control exerted over these flows—are central to understanding which organizations are in positions of power and which are weaker. For community foundations, the quest for endowment gifts is the driving concern of administrators. Without resources, the mission of the foundation cannot be pursued. What community foundations do under such constraints is commit significant resources, both in terms of staff time and administrative expenses, to fundraising. Community foundations also frequently pursue high-profile grantmaking, like funding public radio and television, in order to gain publicity and increase their profile within the community. On the staffing side, someone must be focused on securing new gifts.

The Greater Kansas City Community Foundation, for example, has full-time staff members whose sole function is to solicit contributions to the foundation and manage relations with donors. To encourage donations, the foundation has initiated a range of programs that make contributing to this community foundation an attractive alternative to setting up an independent foundation. First, the foundation allows contributors to maintain considerable control over the disbursement of grants generated by their gifts. These "donor-advised" funds create significant accounting complexities, since many of the funds within the foundation must be tracked and administered separately. Donor-advised funds also undermine to some extent the foundation's ability to control its own grantmaking programs. Catering to donors' desire to have some control over their gifts after they have been made has paid off well, however, for the Greater Kansas City Community Foundation: it has been able to counter the trend toward greater giving through new vehicles by making the community foundation form appealing to donors who want to take an active role in disbursing their philanthropic resources.

Community foundations are often able to attract donors by offering themselves up as hosts for family philanthropy. Donors also have used a community foundation to house their own family foundations as "supporting organizations," which allow families to have their own board of trustees (usually with minority board representation from the sponsoring community foundation) and carry out philanthropy in a group fashion. While organized and run like family foundations, supporting organizations within a community foundation can avoid a lot of the paperwork associated with independence and rely instead on the structure and support of the community foundation in administrative matters. However, just as with donor-advised funds, community foundations are rarely able to exert much control over the direction of these supporting organizations or integrate them into a broader, community foundation–driven philanthropic agenda.

Resource-dependence theory illuminates the way power in community foundations is shaped by relations with outside donors. Community foundations engage in a complex game of courting and supporting current and new donors, which places those who give in a position of considerable power. Donors now exert substantial influence through the establishment of donor-advised funds, which represent an ever-larger percentage of giving to community foundations. Whether pursuing unrestricted gifts, donor-advised funds, or supporting funds, community foundations are similar to universities and other nonprofit organizations that must solicit funds: the money chase invariably leads to a loss of at least some autonomy. Decisions are not made solely on the basis of merit and need, but instead on the way gifts will appeal to important donors or potential donors.

CORPORATE FOUNDATIONS

Corporate foundations operate much the same way as private foundations, with one large exception. While a few corporate foundations have modest endowments, most operate with few or no resources committed in perpetuity to charitable causes. Most corporations make annual contributions to their foundations based on a percentage of profits. To be sure, there is usually a small reserve fund maintained to pay administrative expenses and make emergency grants. But this amount pales in comparison to the multibillion-dollar cash reserves of many large private foundations. Because the annual grants of a corporate foundation are linked more or less directly to the performance of the firm, substantial fluctuation in the level of charitable giving occurs from year to year as market conditions change. There is more than a little irony in this aspect of corporate giving: when recessions hit the nation, corporations almost always are forced to scale back their charitable activity—a reduction that occurs precisely when grants are most urgently needed by nonprofit service agencies. As some corporate foundations manage to persist while others die or fade from prominence, the landscape of corporate philanthropy changes. The fact that corporate philanthropy is shaped by the competitive position of firms ultimately defines the unique character of this form of philanthropic activity.

Because of their unique ties to market competition among firms, corporate foundations can be usefully understood by using the tools of population ecology. Population ecology looks at the development of groups of organizations and emphasizes the role that natural selection plays in organizational dynamics. The ecological perspective rests on the notion that organizations are not maximizers capable of swift and rational adaptation to the environment. Instead, organizations are beholden to standard operating procedures and have limited ability to collect and digest information in the face of powerful environmental forces. Organizational inertia—stemming from bounded rationality, sunk costs, and turnaround time—may make it impossible for organizations to react to change quickly enough to meet new environmental demands. Accordingly, organizations are not always able to search out optimal solutions to the never-ending stream of environmental challenges that arise. Plus, there are powerful forces that weigh against adaptation: change often produces inefficiencies that may weaken a firm's competitive position, gained through economies of scale and well-established procedures. Moreover, there is the liability of newness, which makes change difficult in a turbulent environment. For these reasons, populations of organizations are often helpless in the face of selection pressures that stem from environmental demands.

The lack of substantial endowments in corporate philanthropy means that an important buffer between philanthropy and the prevailing economic trends has been removed. Not only are corporate foundations sensitive to changes in the economic environment, but they must also be sensitive to the interests of the corporate sponsor. Corporate foundations cannot and do not make grants in an arbitrary fashion: every grant usually has some instrumental value, even if this value is relatively small. The growth of corporate philanthropy over the past decades is the product of a growing sense that it is good business to give something back to the communities in which a corporation operates. Indeed, corporate foundations invest substantially in measuring the impact of their giving on the health of their business. Thus, for example, while the Dow Chemical Company Foundation has a broad range of philanthropic interests, it does spend a good deal of money on improving science education for minorities. Students receiving Dow scholarships are then invited to intern at the company and are recruited into the company after graduation. More often, however, corporate self-interest is simply shaped by geography: firms tend to do their grantmaking in the cities or regions where they operate, with the simple goal of building goodwill and appearing as good corporate citizens.

For the individual donor, the question of whether to use a corporate foundation only arises when the donor has a corporate or business interest large enough to make this possible. Corporate foundations can enhance the reputation and community standing of the company, but may not reflect as directly on the donor. For this reason, corporate giving programs tend not to be substitutes for the other forms of individual philanthropy, but rather an additional vehicle through which charitable impulses can be channeled.

One of the most distinguishing features of private or independent foundations is their ability to function and survive regardless of the environment around them. Since they are endowed and do not seek additional funds, private foundations have a unique level of independence. Private foundations are not beholden to outside groups for needed resources, nor are these foundations subject to competitive pressures to locate a market niche in order to survive. On the contrary, private foundations have a position of independence from which they can experiment in ways that are impossible in the public sector or in the business world. What then shapes the action of private foundations? What is the defining element of their organizational form? I argue here that it is the quest for legitimacy and the emergence of strong professional norms that have been the key feature of American private foundations. One tool for understanding these features is the new institutionalism in organizational analysis.

In its present form, the new institutionalism in organizational analysis is a big tent, which accommodates a broad range of theoretical, methodological, and substantive interests. Differences among institutional arguments are considerable, but a few central issues and themes do unite the approach. In its broadest sense, institutionalism argues that organizations are driven by outside pressures to legitimize their work, professionalize the workplace, and copy what other organizations are doing. With its emphasis on legitimacy, satisficing behavior, and symbols, institutionalism presents a major departure from such rival theories as transaction costs economics, population ecology, and resource-dependence theory. Neo-institutionalism emphasizes the role external coercion plays in shaping organizations. The coercive pressures that drive organizations to adopt legitimized practices come mostly from external sources connected to the state, such as regulatory, licensing, and accrediting agencies. Once new practices are adopted by a few organizations working in a common area or field, these "ways of doing things" spread among similar organizations, as the desire to fit in and avoid further conflict with the environment increases. The pressure to conform and the need for legitimacy ultimately lead to isomorphism and homogenization within fields. With its emphasis on symbols and legitimacy, neo-institutionalism has often been described as representing a radical and complete rejection of rational action theory, which uses utility maximization as its touchstone.

Private foundations have long engaged in many of the highly symbolic and ritualistic behaviors that neo-institutionalism predicts. Large private foundations have elaborate financial accounting systems, structured evaluations of their grantmaking programs, and a whole host of other internal controls aimed at making the foundations appear well managed and accountable. Many of these behaviors are just as much aimed at building public support and legitimacy as they are at meeting real-world management needs. Indeed, philanthropy is an amazingly simple activity that has been complicated by the drive of foundations to demonstrate that the tax-exemption status these institutions enjoy is deserved. There is a profound decoupling within many foundations between the internal management practices and the intended goals of the organization. Many times, layer upon layer of controls—over grantmaking decisions and over financial strategy—are instituted to ensure that legitimacy and public confidence are maintained. This is an ironic development, given that freedom from constraints that burden both government and business enterprises is one of the oldest justifications of private philanthropy.

Bureaucracy in philanthropy also tends to produce compromises and safe decisions. As decisions are reviewed over and over again, most controversial and risky grant applications are rejected. The grants are thus filtered to such an extent that little emerges at the end of the decision-making chain that anyone could possibly find objectionable. The sanitizing of all decisions through bureaucratic structures is also ironic given that philanthropy has traditionally prided itself in being innovative and experimental, thus willing to fund solutions to social problems that others would not.

While bureaucratization and professionalization have hit most of America's largest private foundations over time, the last two decades have seen the rapid spread of these processes to foundations with only modest resources. Among large private foundations, the MacArthur Foundation, with assets of over $3 billion, has been subject to profound isomorphic transformation and professionalization. MacArthur's administrative staff has grown exponentially during its first two decades of operation. When John D. MacArthur died and left his fortune to the foundation, a minuscule staff was hired to administer the foundation. The board of directors made many of the grantmaking decisions, and the staff simply processed the paperwork and issued the checks. But over the years, the foundation has grown to over two hundred employees, possesses a large downtown office building, and enjoys every technical amenity and luxury one would find in a major corporation. Administrative expenses at MacArthur, particularly staff salaries, are high and have even been the subject of criticism for diverting too many resources to non-charitable purposes. By creating multiple layers of professional staff to support its grantmaking work, the MacArthur Foundation and other large private foundations have succeeded in legitimizing themselves and making their decisions appear to be less a function of board interests and values, and more a function of comprehensive and fair review by professional staff.

Many of the central tenets of neo-institutionalism have clear application to private foundations: the return to legitimacy as a central organizational problem, the emphasis on structural decoupling, and the tendency toward isomorphism within fields. While institutionalism has been criticized as seeing all organizational behavior as symbolic rather than purposeful, the theory remains a good tool for understanding the structure and practices of private foundations. As one of the few organizational forms that are forever resource-independent, private foundations enjoy both the freedom that endowments provide as well as the buffering that shields these institutions from pressures to perform.

Connecting Theories

So far, philanthropy's four forms and functions have been neatly aligned with the four classic explanations of the behavior of organizations. While this approach draws out the central feature of each organizational form, it obscures the connections between the forms. Although the four types of foundations may appear substantially different in structure and in mission, a number of parallels and similarities actually exist. The association of a theory with a particular organizational form is limiting, in that it chooses to overlook the explanatory value of rival theories for each of the different forms. Thus, for example, resource dependence may well capture the most central assumption of community foundations, namely, the need to attract resources from local donors. But community foundations also require legitimacy, in that the flow of contributions to the endowment is contingent on the foundation being perceived as fulfilling the community's interests. At the same time, community foundations in the same geographical region can be seen as locked in a competitive struggle with one another for a philanthropic niche: community foundations define their missions in a variety of ways, each with a different target population of donors and each directed at building assets and increasing grants. Other parallels between the forms can also be drawn.

In the end, the juxtaposition of organization theory and philanthropy may be a handy antidote to the current overabundance of historical studies of the evolution of organized giving. Many researchers have provided credible accounts of why private foundations and operating foundations were created around the turn of the century, and why corporate foundations and community foundations emerged as major philanthropic players soon thereafter. No matter how detailed these accounts have been in terms of historical facts, they have succeeded in illuminating only part of the picture.

For the emergence and spread of philanthropic forms have not been driven exclusively by the convergence of social forces or events. The historian is ultimately ill equipped to explain the endurance of organizational forms over time. Drawing on the tools of organization theory, I have suggested that philanthropy's four main forms emerged and continue to find currency because each represents a different strategic response to a combination of internal management challenges and external demands.

Philanthropy's four main forms have emerged not simply because of the convergence of historical factors, but because each form has presented a strategic option that is more or less appealing, according to a donor's philanthropic intent and resources. Depending on the narrowness or breadth of their philanthropic intent and shaped by the amount of resources available for charitable purposes, donors have chosen different paths. When they have put a premium on name recognition and lacked a single clear philanthropic intent, many have chosen to start private foundations. When their resources have not quite been sufficient to justify setting up a private foundation, many have made gifts to community foundations. When the charitable mission has been well defined and when it can best be pursued through foundation-administered programs, many donors have decided to create operating foundations. Corporations acting as donors have chosen to start corporate foundations for similarly strategic reasons as individual donors, often opting to set up foundations rather than administer ad hoc giving programs after reaching a certain level of size and stability.

The ability of these four distinct organizational forms to cope with a variety of internal management challenges and external environmental pressures will ensure the long-term viability of the field, particularly if major individual donors continue to turn in large numbers to foundations to execute their long-term philanthropic visions. For as donors search for vehicles to fulfill their diverse charitable intentions, the existence of philanthropy's four main forms ensures that a viable organizational solution will always be present. Choice among the main forms will be a function to some extent of the priorities and needs of the donors, and the match of the institutional structure to the broader strategic direction that is pursued.

Additional Vehicles

FAMILY FOUNDATIONS

One of the most popular variations on the four main institutional forms is the family foundation, which is identical to the private foundation with two major exceptions: it is governed by family members, and its goals include both grantmaking and the enactment and inculcation of values across generations through family giving. The boundary line between an independent foundation and a family foundation is nebulous, although it might be simplest to define a family foundation as one in which the descendants of the founding donor control a majority of the board. Beyond this basic characteristic, there are considerable variations between family foundations that are professionally staffed and managed, such as the Surdna Foundation in New York City, which is still controlled by the Andrus family (Surdna is Andrus spelled backward), and family foundations that are unstaffed and run informally by a group of relatives who come together to talk about social issues and purposes. One of the many arguments for family foundations is that they provide a vehicle for keeping relatives talking and working together, while also teaching the values of service and generosity. Donors are drawn to family foundations because they appear to be a tool for bridging differences, teaching about money, and building social consciences in the young.

Not all plans for family unity and learning through philanthropy are realized. J. M. Kaplan founded the J.M. Kaplan Fund with little experience in philanthropy. He built up his fortune from nothing, eventually amassing over $100 million from his leadership of the Welch's grape juice corporation. Kaplan greatly admired families such as the Rockefeller clan, but by the account of his own heirs, Kaplan did not have a clear ideology of what he wanted his foundation to aggressively pursue. His grandson Matt Davidson, who served as executor of the estate, noted that if somebody came to Kaplan and he took a liking to that person, he would fund their project. Kaplan's giving was very much a direct response to an immediate impression. There was no real definition or program to the philanthropy. Kaplan's children and his grandchildren served on the fund's board but were plagued with the challenges of weak governance structures and an unclear programmatic mandate. After Kaplan passed away, the heirs to his fund have found it increasingly difficult to work together as they have moved away from New York and become attracted to diverse and contradictory causes.

When J. M. Kaplan gave up control of grant and program management in 1977, the leadership job went to one of his four children, Joan Davidson. She established the fund's long-term commitment to New York City "livability." The Kaplan Fund has been widely recognized for signature initiatives in historic preservation and parks and arts funding in New York City. There was some dissension among Kaplan's children about Joan's strong leadership. Some complained that Kaplan put Joan in charge to offset her disappointment after losing a post in the state government. Joan's three siblings sat on the board of trustees but were reduced to rubber-stamping her decisions. As another generation of Kaplan's descendants became involved with the fund, the problem of a unified purpose worsened. The Kaplan Fund's mission was unclear from the start. To make matters worse, Kaplan gave mixed signals on his intent for the fund as he approached death. At times he talked about dissolving the foundation within ten years. At other times he told people that he could see the foundation going on forever as a way of preserving family unity. After Kaplan's death in 1987, the foundation started coming apart at the seams. Davidson gave up her role, and professional help was brought in to get the foundation back on track.

Divisions were hard to overcome. The board was eventually divided into two groups. One group consisted of J. M. Kaplan's four children. They were given control of 35 percent of the grant budget and could each make about $450,000 in grants annually. The second group consisted of the second generation of Kaplan heirs. They could make grants by consensus and also could each award up to $25,000 in trustee-initiated grants. If Kaplan's intent as a donor was for the fund to bring his heirs into a working relationship and enforce family unity, then the fund has been a hopeless failure from the start. The first group of heirs has always been divided, and giving each of the four children their own funds to disburse has failed to bring any unity. The second generation briefly considered just splitting their annual budget eight ways, but ultimately decided against individual grants in favor of consensus-based grants, spearheaded by the foundation staff, focusing primarily on their interpretation of the fund's main issue area, livability in New York City. The ability of this group to abandon its pet interests for the sake of coherence can be viewed as a victory for professional grantmaking, but it did lead to general apathy among the younger generation. In the name of focus and impact, the group gave up their private passions and their ability to use philanthropy to act on their personal commitments and convictions. The result was that the fund had a credible program, but few of the board members were interested in it. As staff took on greater responsibilities, some board members lost interest in attending and thought the process was now out of their hands.

The Kaplan Fund's experience with family philanthropy is instructive because it highlights the enduring tension between private values and public purposes. Being able to express and enact one's values is critical to donor satisfaction. This is what the first generation of Kaplans has chosen to do, and all four family members seem quite satisfied, even if the collective impact and significance of their giving is not readily apparent. The second generation has chosen to focus on the other half of the philanthropic equation, namely, the orderly pursuit of meaningful public purposes. The younger Kaplans have not experienced the same level of satisfaction as the older generation has in part because they have willingly sublimated their personal interests and passions in order to achieve a measure of professionalism, focus, and order to their group giving.

Family foundations are useful vehicles for donors to consider, although, as the Kaplan family's experience highlights, achieving some kind of strategic fit between private values and public purposes can be difficult when family dynamics and family issues are added to the already contentious issues of how to give charitable funds away responsibly.

FEDERATIONS

Federations are another long-standing option to donors seeking a vehicle through which to carry out their giving. Ranging from the secular federations such as the United Way to the more religiously grounded such as the Jewish Federations, donors seeking assistance in making the right choices about what causes to support have options that require little effort. Federations will often approach donors through various campaigns and seek a contribution with the promise to disburse the funds raised to worthy causes and organizations. At the core of the federated giving model is the argument that funds pooled together can have a greater impact and that expert selection of recipient organizations can lead to greater community benefits. Federations also create a sense of solidarity among those who give, particularly in the workplace settings where the United Way, for example, focuses. Giving can become the norm, and a friendly competition between groups can emerge to see who can deliver the greatest cumulative gift to a specific federated campaign.

While this simple vehicle is appealing to smaller donors, major donors have begun to ask why they need such intermediaries as federations to filter their giving. They have fallen on somewhat harder times lately when it comes to major donors. The whole process of disintermediation, which swept through the financial industry and led to millions of individuals taking control of their own investments, has found a correlate in the world of philanthropy. Shaken by a series of scandals involving mismanagement and fraud, the United Way has struggled in recent years to regain its footing and the confidence of donors. As a result, federations are no longer viewed as the logical and inevitable vehicle through which young donors will make their gifts, and their claim of expert knowledge has been effectively challenged by a new generation of givers that is willing and interested in getting more engaged with philanthropic decision making.

GIFT FUNDS

One of the newest vehicles open to donors is the product of large mutual fund companies, which have become eager to meet not only the investment needs of clients but their philanthropic needs as well. Rather than sit idly by as philanthropic funds are transferred out of mutual fund accounts into family and community foundations, several large firms have established their own charitable organizations that act in many ways like community foundations, although they often offer reduced fees, practically no regulations, and less paperwork than many other vehicles. Gift funds have attracted billions of dollars in a very short period of time. One reason for their surging popularity is that they speak directly to the desire of donors to make their own charitable decisions. Gift funds simply take the names of the organizations submitted by donors, check their tax-exempt status, and then send a check in the amount specified by the donor. These funds typically operate with lower expenses than community foundations, a fact that has caused some in the foundation community to worry about this new competition. In many ways, gift funds represent a clear response to the desire of some donors for efficient support for philanthropy that focuses on the mechanics rather than the substance of giving. Gift funds also mirror the broader trend in the financial services industry toward disintermediation and the empowerment of the customer as chief decision maker and strategist.

The community foundation world has not greeted the emergence of this new vehicle warmly. In fact, for several years, leaders of the community foundation field lobbied and worked through the media in an attempt to close down these funds. One reason the established community foundations felt threatened by the gift funds was the perceived lower costs associated with having a financial services company, not a nonprofit, administer a donor-advised fund. In fact, when Fidelity Investments' costs are compared to those of full-service community foundations, the comparisons are not always flattering. Beyond the question of fees, the gift funds were a threatening development because they represented a complete repudiation of the idea that foundation professionals added value. The gift funds presented their services as a more efficient solution for donors seeking to make their own charitable decisions.

INTERNET FOUNDATIONS

For donors not wanting to place their funds into any kind of institutional resting place on the way to disbursal, a range of intermediary institutions for channeling funds directly to causes have emerged. The philanthropic landscape has seen the emergence of a host of new Internet-based virtual foundations that connect causes to donors. These institutions operate mainly online. One example of a charitable cause finding its way to a new audience is Schooling for Children in Matopeni, Kenya, a program designed to increase literacy and life chances for the poor in Africa.

Education donors can make their gifts through the Virtual Foundation, which encourages small-scale giving by individuals in support of grassroots projects in the fields of environment, health, and sustainable development. Though the gifts are often small in scale, the Virtual Foundation allows for otherwise improbable connections between donors and nonprofits. The Virtual Foundation is a project of ECOLOGIA (Ecologists Linked for Organizing Grassroots Initiatives and Action), an organization that provides technical support and training to grassroots environmental efforts worldwide. Given its global perspective, ECOLOGIA is also able to connect individuals and organizations that might share information and resources to improve their local efforts. The Virtual Foundation allows donors to take advantage of ECOLOGIA's global network of grass-roots environmentalism. Projects seeking funding through the Virtual Foundation must first meet approval with a local intermediary organization—there are thirty worldwide—that recommends projects to the Virtual Foundation. Once the Virtual Foundation approves a project, it is posted on the website with a description and budget. The ultimate screening process, of course, is left to the donor who chooses to contribute. For a donor interested in making a small gift to a local organization in another part of the world, the Virtual Foundation model is ideal.

DONOR NETWORKS

While the Virtual Foundation seeks very small contributions to support small projects around the world, other groups, like the Acumen Fund, seek much larger commitments. The Acumen Fund adopts many of the principles of venture capitalism and applies them to the world of international grantmaking. It seeks partners who will give—or "invest"—$100,000 in one of several grantmaking portfolios, including health technology, economic development, and water resources. Using expert advisors in these fields, the fund selects and features a small group of projects that meet a set of criteria, including whether the project meets an unmet need, has an innovative approach with the potential for broad impact, has strong leadership, and has a plan for long-term sustainability. Its work includes the distribution of long-lasting anti-malaria bed nets in Africa, the building of affordable housing in Pakistan, and the implementation of new drip irrigation systems in India. Contributors to the fund get regular updates on the progress of the projects they have chosen to support and access to special events and travel opportunities to visit the supported projects. The fund charges donors a fee of 10 percent of their contributions for these services. The Acumen Fund thus has features of a virtual foundation, a community foundation, and a membership organization.

Donors do not come together just to get the best possible expert advice to guide their philanthropy. Sometimes they seek out a connection related to philanthropy with broader purposes in mind. One such multipurpose group, Mama Cash, was founded in the Netherlands, and it seeks to protect and expand women's rights and opportunities across the globe. With individual and foundation support, the group invests in women-initiated projects to protect women from violence, promote women's art, support economic equality, fight homophobia, and work for peace. Five women started Mama Cash in 1983 as an expressly radical funding organization. One Mama Cash initiative, called Women with Inherited Wealth, is a network of female inheritors in the Netherlands. The operating assumptions of the effort are that money that one inherits is not the same as money that one earns, and that often there are conditions attached to inherited wealth. To overcome these obstacles, the organization assists women in safely navigating their way through what they see as a male-dominated, conservative financial world. The goal of this network is to increase the self-confidence of women so that they can take full responsibility for their inherited wealth and to encourage them to use their inheritance in a socially responsible manner. This approach to educating donors is about more than helping women make smart philanthropic decisions. The feminist perspective of Women with Inherited Wealth assumes that a woman faces inherent obstacles when dealing with money, and that philanthropy can be a tool to explore one's values and set a life direction.

Another new vehicle is giving circles, the joining together of donors into local clubs that act as one in doing philanthropy. Giving circles are based on the belief that donors want to embed giving in the process of forging social ties among individuals. Giving circles are vehicles that are particularly attractive to donors who want company as they make their philanthropic journeys. Typically, such groups are local coalitions and networks of individuals that support local causes. The Hestia Fund in Boston, for example, is a group of women that seeks to pool funds and work together to find worthwhile projects. With an evolving membership of about forty members each giving $5,000, the group works with local charities on issues of concern to the group, usually in and around the Boston area so that participants can see firsthand how their funds are used.

CHARITABLE TRUSTS

Donors seeking some combination of income and estate tax reduction have a range of planned giving options open to them. When Jacqueline Kennedy Onassis died, much of her estate went into a charitable lead trust, which permitted both her heirs and the selected charities to receive a significantly larger portion of her estate than would otherwise have been possible because of estate taxes. The benefits of a charitable trust are not limited, however, to the glamorous and most affluent. Charitable trusts can be important vehicles through which to accomplish more modest philanthropic objectives. They permit an individual to make substantial gifts to a favorite charitable organization without giving up all rights over the property either currently or at a later time. Through a charitable trust, an individual can make an irrevocable future gift to a charity and still claim a current income tax deduction for the gift.

Trusts are often the product of both careful estate planning and the pursuit of charitable purposes. Charitable trusts come in two main forms: the charitable lead trust and the charitable remainder trust. The mechanics of these trusts are fairly straightforward. A charitable lead trust delivers a stream of income for a set period of years to the designated nonprofit organization. When the period is over, the property held in trust returns to the donor or to a beneficiary designated by the donor. The operating principle is thus one of giving away funds over time, resulting in a tax-advantaged transfer of the remaining assets at a later date. Under a charitable lead trust, the donor receives an immediate federal income tax deduction when making the gift, equal to the present value of the future income stream. The donor is taxed each year, however, on the value of the income interest that is payable to the charity. A donor may set up a charitable lead trust while alive or at death through instructions in a will, with the assets returning years later to the heirs that the donor designates. Another option, a charitable remainder trust, allows a stream of income to reach the donor for a specified period of time, which is often defined as the donor's lifetime. At the conclusion of this time period, a gift of the assets is made to a charity.

Alignment and Fit

In evaluating the ample array of options for philanthropic vehicles available today, donors need to pay special attention to the mission that is being pursued, the appropriate time frame for the giving, and the grantmaking style sought by the donor. Selecting the appropriate structure through which to give requires a conscious effort aimed at overall fit and alignment. While choosing an appropriate philanthropic vehicle must be integrated into the broader task of setting a coherent philanthropic direction, a few key questions must be considered before working on alignment and fit.

One way to think about the many options available to donors is to array the institutional landscape of philanthropy along two major dimensions of concern to donors: the specificity of the mission to be pursued and the amount of donor resources available for philanthropy (see fig. 6.1). These two considerations will of course vary greatly from donor to donor.

In surveying this space and the options contained therein, donors face a number of challenges. The first is that their philanthropic intentions may not be static, but dynamic. In fact, donors' interests will likely evolve as time passes. Many major donors have spent the vast majority of their time and effort building successful businesses and have not really been able to focus on the question of what issues and causes excite their passions. One donor likes to tell the story of working so hard at a software start-up business that he was stunned to learn, when looking at the receipt from an ATM, that his personal checking account had $6 million in it. Up until then,

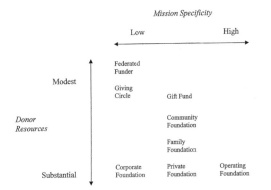

Fig. 6.1: Selected institutional options for individual donors.

he knew he was making money, but he had no real sense of the scale. As the amount escalated quickly, especially after the sale of the company, the entrepreneur knew it was time to find some real productive use for these funds and has since thrown himself into philanthropy as a full-time occupation. Some donors think about philanthropy a lot while making money and have strong opinions from the outset, but then lose interest once the reality of seeking to address a particularly difficult social problem becomes clearer through philanthropic experience. For these donors, philanthropic focus can go from very clear to nebulous in a short period of time. The problem with either of these natural shifts is that they can confound and render problematic the choice of philanthropic institution or vehicle. And it may not be just the underlying purposes and objectives that change; it can be the time frame of the donor, the personal style of the donor, or other factors.

One way to address the challenge of achieving fit and alignment between vehicle and philanthropic purposes is for donors to have multiple vehicles at their disposal. While there are some considerations related to ease of use, overhead expenses, and resource dispersal, donors can call on multiple vehicles to meet their complex interests and needs. Thus, a donor may want to take part in a giving circle in order to enjoy the benefits of peer learning and network building, while also having a donor-advised fund in a community foundation or a family foundation. Or a donor may set up a private foundation to make grants in a particular field or area with the benefit of advice and counsel from staff and other trustees, but also choose to have a gift fund at a brokerage house in order to support a favorite set of charities that are well known to the donor, such as an alma mater, a hospital, or groups that have special personal meaning. Vehicles for giving do not require exclusive commitments, and they can be used in combination to create a portfolio of instruments.

Nevertheless, one important consideration arises related to philanthropic vehicles, particularly with private and operating foundations: they tend to be harder to alter than any of the other elements that make up the philanthropic prism. Changing the stated mission of a private foundation dramatically from what is spelled out in the original filings can be an expensive and time-consuming matter, demanding expert legal advice and even the consent of state charity regulators. While it has certainly been accomplished, such efforts at mission redefinition must usually first demonstrate that the original mission is impractical, inefficient, or impossible to accomplish. Because of the safeguards set up to protect the intent of the donor after funds are placed into foundations, many donors define their philanthropic intentions in very broad terms when creating a perpetual foundation, even when they have a good sense of the direction they want to pursue in the short run. Changes in missions are rendered difficult in perpetual foundations not only by the legal barriers that must be overcome: just as significant is the problem of placating nonprofit organizations and other stakeholders following a change in focus that renders existing grantees ineligible for future funding. Mission changes in foundations create winners, losers, and strife.

Donors or their families may also change their minds about the amount of involvement they want. In Chicago, the descendants of pharmaceuticals magnate Gideon Daniel Searle eventually sued the Chicago Community Trust in order to get greater control over the actual choice of causes that the family's $250 million trust would support. While the founder thought the choice of a community foundation appropriate and a good fit with his philanthropic interests, those who followed did not and sought successfully through a three-year legal battle to get a modification that would allow the family greater say in what kinds of grants are made with the funds donated by Searle. In other instances, donors have started off believing that they wanted a deep engagement and involvement with philanthropy, only to learn through experience that a different style is appropriate. For these donors, creating an operating foundation requiring large amounts of hands-on work can be a major false step.

While almost all the mistakes donors make related to their choice of vehicles for their giving are reversible, having much of the broader strategic mix well-defined first is wise. Selecting an institutional vehicle first is possible but may have real costs if the other elements of strategic giving have not been given careful attention. With little reason to make this kind of commitment quickly and with much flexibility preserved by direct giving, donors need to locate a compelling and lasting rationale for a decision to shift to a philanthropic vehicle or combination of vehicles. While there can be peer pressure in elite circles to either form a family foundation or to set up a donor-advised fund or even to join a giving circle, these sorts of commitments should never be driven by trends or concern over appearances. Only when the vehicle of choice for giving is well fitted to the mission that is selected, the kind of change that will be pursued, the donor's own identity, and a defensible time frame will the move to institutional giving contribute to rather than detract from the ability of donors to produce value through their giving.

CHAPTER SEVEN

Toward Strategic Giving

One of the challenges in exploring the nature of philanthropic strategy is that giving has so many different forms, ambitions, and ideals. Philanthropy lacks the coherence of a traditional occupation or field because it still operates largely without a settled doctrine or a set of accepted practices. In fact, one of the most interesting features of philanthropy is that it is practiced not only by a homogeneous group of wealthy elites, but by people from all walks of life. Donors come to giving with a huge range of life experiences, which in turn shape their philanthropic objectives. The purposes and values expressed through philanthropy by individual donors, and to a lesser extent by institutional donors, are translated into a patch quilt of good work, with plenty of room for disagreement about substance and methods.

The framework presented in this book is neutral on core substantive issues, but does point to five questions that donors need to confront as they begin to chart their philanthropic plans. What is valuable to my community and me? What kinds of nonprofit activity will work best? What vehicle can best be used to accomplish my goals? When should my giving take place? What level of engagement and visibility do I want for my giving? When each question is posed independently, I have argued that there are no universally appropriate answers to any one of these five questions. There are, however, sets of responses that coalesce more or less well together. This points to the following basic premise: Strategic giving should be understood as the alignment of the five core philanthropic dimensions (see fig. 7.1). When answers to all five questions fit well together, the probability of achieving the desired public impact and satisfying the donors' underlying needs are high. Achieving fit or alignment is also a critical step in the move toward the more effective, accountable, and legitimate exercise of philanthropic power.

While all five elements of the philanthropic prism must be brought into focus together, clear exposition has required that the elements be defined and developed independently in the previous five chapters. The flaw in this mode of presentation is that it works to some extent against the underlying claim and argument, namely that the essence of strategy consists in the achievement of fit, alignment, and coherence among all five of the critical elements. Another problem with this presentation is that the elements examined early on may wrongly appear more central than those considered later. Yet, just as I claimed at the outset of the book, it is possible to engage the challenge of philanthropy by starting with a commitment to any one or more elements of the prism and then elaborating and filling in the rest. It would be a mistake not to take advantage of this flexibility because so much of strategy in philanthropy is personal and dependent on the sometimes very distinctive and often inscrutable motives of donors.

How can one really know whether alignment has been achieved? One way is to take seriously the challenge to measure both mission effectiveness (how well the funder is doing at achieving its mission) and program effectiveness (how well nonprofits are doing at achieving their goals). Having good information about both aspects of philanthropic performance could in principle be very valuable to donors. It could allow for growth and learning over time and help a donor get better at the work of giving. While it never has existed in practice, imagine what a fully functional performance measure-

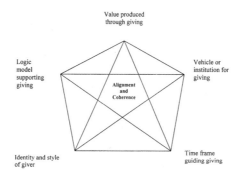

Value produced
through giving

Logic
model
supporting
giving

Vehicle or
institution for
giving

Alignment
and
Coherence

Identity and style
of giver

Time frame
guiding giving

Fig. 7.1: Alignment and coherence in the philanthropic prism.

ment system in philanthropy might look like: a donor could look up any nonprofit organization and find a detailed report on the programs carried out by the group, with their impact on the community measured with sensible indicators, and a series of scores that would allow the donor to assess the quality of one group's work compared to that of other organizations working in the same field. Such a system has never existed and likely will never be seen by donors. It is a fiction because so many of the dimensions of charitable activity cannot be clearly measured, because results are almost always incommensurable across organizations and across fields, and because the cost of developing and maintaining such a system would be too high. What then is a donor to do? The answer lies in the search for imperfect but usable knowledge and the cultivation of the capacity to learn over time. The use of performance data to guide philanthropy is appealing because it promises to bring some reason and method to a world of giving that sometimes is driven mainly by reaction and impulse.

Functions and Forms of Evaluation

Donors are in a position to do three important things through measurement. First, they may be able to improve overall program performance. In principle, the use of evaluation research can help donors adjust and restructure nonprofit programs so that they have a higher probability of success. Funders are in a position of power—in that they control the flow of funds—and this permits them to insist on programmatic changes should evaluation data so indicate. After a particular program is complete, the use of program evaluations can allow donors to design and fund better programs. The operational applications of performance data can be directed inward as well. Through studies of their own grantmaking procedures and systems, institutional donors in particular have been able to improve the overall operational efficiency of their grantmaking, all with an eye to making their otherwise forbidding institutions more approachable and easier to work with. In this way, evaluation research can help donors both improve nonprofit operations and their own philanthropic operations.

The second use of evaluation research in philanthropy is connected to the political and authorizing environment. At a time when funds for discretionary program spending are increasingly limited, the ability of donors to document programmatic success can be a potent tool for mobilizing political support for further public funding for effective recipient organizations. Evaluation research also allows donors to make the case for additional private support by other donors interested in the problem or field in question. In addition, meaningful performance data can serve as an umbrella for donors, shielding them from the changes in the political weather around them. Over time, private foundations' assets have proven to be especially frequent and easy targets of Congress and state regulators, who believe these large untapped reserves of funds could be used more aggressively for public purposes. Evaluation data on mission effectiveness of the donor or foundation can be a first line of defense against criticism and calls for increased regulations. Thus, evaluation data can be both a tool for building funding support for the best recipient organizations and an instrument to sustain public and government support of the philanthropy field itself.

The third use of evaluation research is the most important although often the least understood. Collecting, examining, and discussing evaluation research can be an important way of defining and reckoning the philanthropic value to be produced. Working with evaluation data can open up conversations about what is important to measure and, ultimately, what objectives are worth pursuing—both for donors and their recipients. Because evaluations are always about some aspect of performance, they can be tools for articulating and clarifying the nature of the philanthropic value that donors are trying to produce. The act of defining what value is to be achieved can be a focusing exercise for a donor, one that demands that both mission and goals be clearly specified. In the context of foundations, doing this work can be a useful tool for building consensus and solidarity among staff about what the funding is intended to achieve and how any given program will go about achieving results. For individual donors, the process can lead to a greater clarity of purpose and understanding. When the conversation about ultimate purposes takes place within the context of a funded program or initiative, donors and recipients can clarify what ultimately is at stake and worth trying to accomplish. In this sense, defining the core purpose, which is essential if one is to measure whether or not it has been achieved, is a valuable exercise in itself because it cannot help but clarify and render more concrete the ends of philanthropy.

Today measuring is often taken to be an activity designed to track donors' success in achieving their instrumental rather than expressive purposes. Tracking performance is a way of assuring the public that charitable resources are being used wisely and that programs are being operated effectively. The problem with these assumptions about measurement is that they largely ignore the fact that the expressive side of giving—that part of philanthropy by which donors enact their commitments and values—needs to be supported if the flow of funds to charitable purposes is to continue to grow and the field's capacity to innovate and sustain itself is to be enhanced. Evaluations should build universal knowledge that can advance the field's self-understanding, but they should also take seriously the question of how well programs align with the intent and commitments of the funders.

There are at least two ways to go about ensuring that the expressive dimension of giving is part of any evaluation effort being undertaken. The first way is to define the values that are both implicit and explicit in the delivery of a funded program and to compare how close these recipient values are to those of the donor. Some of this work is presumably done before a grant is made. Yet a program could perform well instrumentally by achieving its stated objectives but fail miserably to align with the expressive goals of a funder. Such cases will require tough choices by the donor and the recipient organization about their priorities.

The second way to assess expressive quality of grantmaking is to focus on the funder's work. Turning the evaluation lens inward at the work of giving and the quality of decision making is difficult because it demands both that the values of the donor be made explicit to those carrying out the evaluation and, in the case of professionally managed foundations, that the work of staff be scrutinized in terms of its fidelity to donor intent, rather than to the more accepted standard of effectiveness. Still, the exercise of asking how well a donor or foundation is doing at achieving their mission is valuable if for no other reason than that it refocuses attention on what matters most, namely, the underlying commitments and values that animated the giving in the first place. If evaluation can help do more than just track results and instead help donors see where and how their giving connects with their fundamental beliefs, the field as a whole will likely be significantly strengthened.

The expressive dimension of impact is the easiest to overlook because instrumental goals are both easier to track and fit more closely with the norms of the industry that has established itself around the field. However, a good argument could be made that it is the plurality of values and ideas animating giving that constitute the raison d'être of philanthropy, give it its strength, and justify its special privileged tax status. For this reason, donors should consider focusing carefully on how well the values of the recipient organizations ultimately align with those of the funder. In the end, foundations must make clear decisions about which dimension of impact is most important to them and then seek out the best and most appropriate measurement strategies. To do less is ultimately to fail to act responsibly. After all, donors, nonprofit managers, and policy makers all stand to benefit from honest and open evaluation. If successful in measurement, philanthropy may well begin to define for itself a new and much needed variation on the old Delphic motto "know thyself," one that will stress the importance of the constant search for a better understanding of the many ways that foundations shape society.

Pathways

Much of the discussion here has been about the challenge of constructing and carrying out a philanthropic strategy. This difficult task requires considerable work on the part of the giver. While it is tempting to take the word *strategy* and to conjure up an abstract and disembodied process of careful reflection, giving involves doing just as much as it involves thinking. Of course, the relative mix of thought and action in philanthropy varies considerably from one donor to the next, and, for some donors, from one gift to the next. Still, those who give ultimately seek to improve the effectiveness of their giving, whether it be defined in instrumental or expressive terms or in some combination of the two. The main argument of this book is that building a sound strategy for giving has to be understood as a critical part of the process of moving toward greater levels of effectiveness. Only by getting better at understanding and implementing a strategy for giving will donors be able to produce greater public and private returns over the years. The development of strategy for giving, just like the idea of achieving greater levels of effectiveness, must be understood as an evolutionary process, one that unfolds over time as donors build knowledge and confidence.

If strategy building and improved effectiveness do in fact represent two critical goals that major donors have in mind, one might reasonably ask how the two are related in practice (see fig. 7.2). Here, some difference of opinion exists. One school might argue

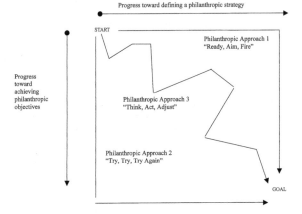

Fig. 7.2: Relationship between philanthropic strategy and philanthropic objectives.

that strategy is ultimately prior to effectiveness, in that donors must have a clear conception of what they are doing for it to have any real chance of succeeding. Taken to an extreme, this approach leads to a kind of conceptual philanthropy, one in which planning and consultation can become cumbersome and extended. Within the world of foundations, this approach—which can be dubbed "Ready, aim, fire" (with a heavy emphasis on the first and second elements)—often spends a large amount of time and resources readying the philanthropic checkbook and aiming the philanthropic sights. Bringing in consultants, talking with experts from academe, comparing notes with other foundations working in the same field, and commissioning white papers that set forward the approach to be taken are all common in foundations that believe in the power of reason and planning. And to some extent, this work can help donors avoid costly and embarrassing mistakes and help ensure that philanthropic funds are introduced only when the terrain has been properly prepared.

For those with an action orientation, a second approach to making philanthropic progress looms larger and more appealing. This more inductive approach to giving holds that most of what is needed to build strategy can only be located in the real world of practice and experience. For these more hardy philanthropic experimenters, the operating mantra is "Try, try, try again," which has a heavy emphasis on repetition. This more experimental and experience-oriented approach to giving is most commonly found in wealthy individual donors who are able to operate without having to seek the approval of a governing board or a professional staff. For the philanthropic principals, learning on the go and making mistakes along the way are the surest ways to arrive at a compelling and battle-tested strategy to guide giving.

Between these two extreme positions, a more sensible middle ground exists, one in which strategy development and progress toward practical objectives unfold in an interactive manner. By making some initial strategic choices, pushing ahead with experiments, considering lessons learned, working to define and refine strategy, and then starting the whole process over again, donors can slowly navigate to a position where significant outcomes are achieved and where a strategy for giving informs philanthropy. This model of philanthropic learning might be termed "Think, act, adjust," although it could just as easily be termed "Act, think, adjust." Getting from the start to the end is an admittedly complex and unpredictable process, which can include both encouraging breakthroughs and disheartening setbacks. However, by adopting an iterative approach to relating strategy and practice, donors are most likely to make progress in both areas. Lessons learned can be used to inform planning and refinements in strategy as well as help advance progress toward objectives.

There are conditions in which it is either inappropriate or impossible to balance strategy and action. One such example is the response to a pressing need or crisis, when, to be useful, philanthropic action must be decisive and speedy. Timing can be critical, with little room for careful strategy formulation. In such cases, donors may need to compromise some short-term effectiveness in the name of responsiveness, and focus on learning on the go. In other instances, when long-term community problems are the subject of the philanthropic intervention, a much more deliberative process may well be in order.

In trying to find the right mix of knowledge and experience, it is useful to recognize that a fair amount of the success of the programs supported by donors comes down to the quality of the person who will actually get the work done. A critical part of being a successful and effective donor thus involves spotting and choosing talented and committed people who can both help devise and effectively implement. When all else fails in the nonprofit sector, the one enduring constant remains that organizations and programs depend on strong leadership and good management. The irony in philanthropy is that much of the system in place focuses on everything but the individual. The grantmaking processes that operate across institutional philanthropy are rarely set up to capture things such as interpersonal skills or value commitment or operational savvy. Rather, a huge amount of weight is placed on the capacity of leaders to produce documents spelling out what they would do if they were given charitable funds. Because success in philanthropy involves progressing along the middle path depicted in figure 7.2, donors benefit greatly when they are able to select and work with the nonprofit leaders who can help navigate this twisting path. In selecting grantees, a key consideration should therefore be the likelihood that the leader of the organization selected will be a productive contributor to the voyage between strategy building and program delivery.

In the end, there is no single solution to the question of how much reason and how much reaction should figure into philanthropy. The mix will depend both on the strategic direction established by the donor and on the problem or issue being tackled. In some cases, such as the crisis after September 11th, there is simply no time to engage in careful planning and systems building. The needs are great and the public pressure for action is so intense that philanthropic reaction will naturally triumph over a reasoned rollout of services. Absent the pressures of crisis response, donors are able to inform decisions about what kinds of programs to implement by drawing on evaluation data of similar efforts that have been implemented in other localities.

By studying what other donors have learned in their work on similar problems in other situations, donors can avoid repeating philanthropic history and reduce—although probably not eliminate—the trial-and-error nature of much of philanthropy. In some human fields, including early childhood development, the amount of data on probable impact and information on program design available is enormous. In other fields, such as youth violence reduction, the data is spottier and often amounts to a few case studies of successful local initiatives. In still other areas, the data is either poor or difficult to apply. Still, knowing something about what others have learned can be valuable to donors starting out in a field. Making strong and sensible linkages among measurement, knowledge building, and ultimately philanthropic action is a challenge. It requires an appreciation of what good evaluation data looks like, an understanding of the limits of evaluation research when it comes to predicting or even informing the future, a willingness to spend money on knowledge building (particularly when the results may be generalizable), and a realistic understanding of the dialectic between strategy building and strategy execution. Donors will make progress toward all these goals by understanding that their giving will inevitably involve the continuous work of strategizing, acting, reacting, measuring, knowing, and adjusting.

The Future of Philanthropy

As donors undertake the work of defining a philanthropic strategy, they should also think carefully about how they understand their roles in the broader social context in which they choose to do their giving as well as their own motives and talents. I have suggested in this book the factors that weigh in favor of a particular perspective on giving, one that seeks to connect the public needs of a community with the private values and commitments of donors. While there is certainly much merit in the idea of philanthropy as a purely productive tool for meeting pressing public needs, I have argued that there is a substantial limitation to this perspective. If philanthropy is nothing more than the quiet and agnostic satisfaction of community needs, it really has not defined for itself a position much different than that of government. And given the capacity of government to raise funds through taxation, philanthropy is not likely to be able to outspend the public sector any time soon, nor mandate that critical changes be achieved. As a consequence, philanthropy is unlikely to really achieve its ultimate potential if all it seeks to do is shadow and supplement public provision.

This leads to the second competing perspective on giving, one that I have tried to emphasize in this book, which starts with a different premise entirely. It holds that only when philanthropy is centered on the personal interests and commitments of donors will philanthropy fulfill its calling to breathe pluralism and innovation into society. Accordingly, philanthropy is best conceived as a private activity that allows donors to use their funds to explore their own private visions of the public good. Rather than apologize for having interests and values, donors should be encouraged to enact these interests and values. Some donors do this by giving to organizations that have played important roles in their lives or in the lives of their family. Others give simply because they identify on a personal level with a particular cause or organization. Not only is giving grounded in values likely to be sustainable over time since it is grounded in lasting human experiences and emotions, but it also stands the best chance of injecting new blood in the field.

Starting from the premise that philanthropy is as much about the donors as it is about the public has radical consequences not only for how one goes about giving, but how one assesses philanthropy and structures public policy to support it. Instead of castigating giving that does not proceed based solely on an analysis of the most urgent human needs, the public may need to be more open to the fact that philanthropy must have a certain autonomy and protection within which donors can operate. To communities in need and nonprofits demanding more funding, this argument will seem a little obscure and even difficult to accept. But it is only necessary to think about the supply of future philanthropic funds to understand why taking seriously the needs and interests of donors is important. Only when donors have the ability to use their philanthropy to do something that is meaningful to them will giving likely flow at high levels. After all, if the choices of donors are subject to endless second-guessing or greater public oversight, the line between private philanthropy and government action will become blurred. It is the donor's ability to direct charitable dollars to causes and organizations that are important to the donor that activates the impulse to give and defines philanthropy's special purpose in a democracy.

The opposition of private values and public purposes that frames too much of our current thinking about philanthropy ultimately rests on a false dichotomy, however. It overlooks the fact that the majority of donors ultimately want to produce both private and public benefits. Success in helping others is often what will give the most satisfaction to donors, since few givers will take any pleasure from giving that fails to achieve its objectives. The political divide that has split philanthropy has made it hard for donors to pursue the most important calling of all: the definition of the points of intersection between their private interests and the public needs. When the donor seeks to both do something that is personally satisfying, while also creating an important benefit for the local community, the task of strategy formulation can require substantial reflection and research. The task of the strategic donor is to work on the *entirety* of the philanthropic prism until each point is defined, polished, and in alignment with the others. Only when donors have achieved this complex and challenging level of fit can they claim that their giving has truly become strategic. Only when giving becomes strategic will donors have a higher probability of creating value for the public and for themselves.

Another recurring theme in this analysis of philanthropy is the importance of human values and convictions to the world of philanthropy. I argued at the outset that the core problems of effectiveness, accountability, and legitimacy have rattled around the world of giving for a long time. I also suggested that the growing professionalization of grantmaking, particularly in the larger foundations, has attempted to address these issues by bringing greater rigor and procedural safeguards to philanthropic decision making and by focusing on the evaluation of grantee organizations. Tightening up philanthropy's front- and back-end processes has allowed some of the larger foundations to claim both increased levels of effectiveness and greater accountability. However, something very important has been neglected in this move. As philanthropic funds have gravitated to private foundations and as donors have over time entrusted their giving to others, a central element in philanthropy has been compromised. The private values, commitments, passions, and perspectives of individual donors have been slowly overwhelmed by more agnostic, uncontroversial, and acceptable procedural values of professional staff. This would not be a problem if philanthropy were simply about the efficient provision of human services. But, again, this is not the case. The fundamental rationale for philanthropy is far broader than simply the channeling of private funds to public purposes. Philanthropy is about pluralism, expression, and innovation just as much as it is about redistribution and change. To justify the whole infrastructure around giving and to deliver fully on its potential contribution to society, philanthropy must strive toward and achieve something far bigger and broader than the competent production of useful goods and services. It must allow individuals to connect their private visions of the public good to real public problems, and, in the process, to enliven the public sphere.

Implicit in my claims about the importance of private values in philanthropy is a concern about the creeping professionalization of giving. As major individual donors choose in large numbers to turn over their wealth to foundations where professional philanthropic managers will decide how best to give far out into the future, something troublesome is occurring. The expressive, impassioned, and opinionated fingerprints of the donor on philanthropy are slowly washed away by time and replaced with more instrumental and neutral philanthropic identities. While grantmaking professionals may have the best of intentions and strive earnestly to achieve the highest value uses of philanthropic funds, something is still lost when the delicate balance of public purposes and private values is tipped in the direction of the former and to the detriment of the latter. Public policy could redress some of this drift by rewarding donors who both act sooner and more decisively when it comes to giving.

Repositioning philanthropy in terms of its expressive and instrumental content—either through changes in public policy or through shifts in the norms within philanthropy—would do a lot to remedy this situation and inject life into the field in the future. There are two reasons that it is in the public interest for philanthropy to validate and reaffirm the private values that individuals are able to bring to giving. The first is that these idiosyncratic and unexpected private formulations of both what items on the public agenda deserve greater attention and how they should best be supported are essential to philanthropy differentiating itself from government. The second argument for a more donor-centered philanthropy is simpler. While the large private foundations occupy a fair amount of the philanthropic limelight, some of the most interesting and provocative giving is likely to be carried by living donors who—unlike their institutional counterparts—are striving albeit imperfectly to craft a legacy for themselves, repay important debts to institutions, build new models for program delivery, and identify a distinctive community need. The sheer complexity of motives and intentions that lie behind individual giving is more likely to lead to provocative ideas and visions than the more straightforward search for effectiveness, accountability, and legitimacy that pervades the world of philanthropic institutions. Finding ways, either through shortened time horizons for giving or through alternative giving vehicles, to empower and encourage principals to act philanthropically, rather than defer key decisions to competent but detached philanthropic agents, is essential to both preserving the vitality of philanthropy and strengthening the role giving plays in society.

Index

operating foundations, 24, 47–49, 130–33, 142; grantmaking in, 133; mission redefinition in, 155–56

opportunity costs, 119–20

organizational forms. *See* institutional forms

organization theory, 142–43

outcomes. *See* effectiveness/efficacy; logic models

Overture Project, 37–39

pace. *See* timing decisions

paradigm production, 58–59, 67–68

Parsons School for Design, 87–88

particularism arguments, 117–18

payout rates, 105–6, 112–18; effectiveness considerations in, 113–15; fairness considerations in, 115–16; value expression of donors in, 116–18

Pelli, Cesar, 38

performance measures, 158–63; of expressive impact, 161–63; function of, 159–61; of funders' work, 162; of instrumental goals, 161–62; of mission effectiveness, 7; of program effectiveness, 6–7; in venture philanthropy, 91, 94–95

perpetuity, 106, 125, 127, 155

Pew Charitable Trusts, 92

philanthropic discounting, 23, 118–24; discount rates in, 119–21; ethical questions in, 122–23

philanthropic prism, 21–24, 157–59, 169. *See also* giving styles; institutional forms; logic models; timing decisions; value parameters

philanthropic value. *See* value parameters

philanthropy, 157–59; as alternative to charity, 2–3; definition of, 5; purposes of, 3–5

pilot programs, 73

pluralism, 4, 118

policy research, 58–59, 67–68

polio programs, 109

political advocacy, 57–58, 160

population ecology, 137–38

power relationships, 99–102

preventive giving, 113–14

private foundations. *See* independent (private) foundations

private values, 30–32, 168–71

process accountability, 8–9

professionalization of philanthropy, x, 139–42, 170–71; *vs.* personal value-driven decisions, 117–18, 145–47, 170–71; value-neutral approach in, 39–40, 77–78, 80–81

profiles of donors, 78, 85–91

program expansion, 70–71

programmatic tactics, 64–68; collaborative integration in, 65–66; commercial ventures in, 66–67; community focus in, 65; creation of new organizations in, 67; government programs in, 66

program-related investments (PRIs), 63

project grants, 62, 92

public education, 57

public profiles of donors, 78, 85–91

public value. *See* value parameters

purposes. *See* value parameters

recognition, 18, 20, 23, 85–91

religious giving, 41–43, 117

replication, 71–75

requests for proposals (RFPs), 63

research grants, 17, 58–59, 67–68

resource-dependence model, 134–36

Robin Hood Foundation, 93

Rockefeller, John D., vii

Rowland, Pleasant, 37

rural poverty, 111

Salamander Inn, 87

Salvation Army, 36

scale, 53–54, 68–75; financial strength in, 68–70; multi-site replication in, 71–75; program expansion in, 70–71

Schooling for Children, 149

scientific philanthropy, 113–14
Searle, Gideon Daniel, 155–56
self-help, 2–3
Sharma, Om Dutta, 89
small donors, 7
Smith, Adam, 132
social (public) needs, 2, 29–31
Social Venture Partners (SVP), 97
specificity of assets, 131–32
strategic giving, vii–ix, 10, 19–26, 157–
    71; alignment in, 24–26, 157–59;
    donor-centered philanthropy in,
    169–71; five core elements (prism)
    of, ix, 20–21, 169; pathways toward
    achievement of, 163–67; performance
    measures in, 159–63; value parame-
    ters of, 45–50, 167–70
style of giving. See giving styles
substantive accountability, 8–9
supporting organizations, 136
Surdna Foundation, 144
Szoka, Cardinal Edmund, 41–42, 43

taking to scale, 68–70, 73–75. See also
    theory of scale
targets of philanthropy, 17
tax considerations, 7, 29–30; of chari-
    table trusts, 130, 152–53; of estate
    taxes, 116, 152; of indirect taxpayer
    subsidies, 116; of tax-exemption
    status, 140
technical assistance, 64, 98–99
Texas (Michener), 82–83
theory of change, 52–60; individual
    training and development in, 54–55;
    network building in, 56–57; organ-
    izational capacity building in, 55–56;
    policy research in, 58–59; political
    engagement in, 57–58; relative effec-
    tiveness in, 59–60
theory of leverage, 22, 53, 54, 61–68;
    grantmaking tactics in, 61–64;
    programmatic tactics in, 64–68
theory of scale, 53–54, 68–75; financial
    strength in, 68–70; multi-site

replication in, 71–75; program
    expansion in, 70–71
Time-Warner, 83–84
timing decisions, ix, 18, 20–21, 23, 105–
    27; in crisis response, 24–25, 111–12,
    166; of do-it-yourself donors, 124–
    25; effectiveness considerations in,
    113–15; in endowment funding, 126;
    fairness considerations of, 115–16,
    122–23; geographical boundaries in,
    112–13; payout rates in, 105–6, 112–
    18, 127; perpetuity option in, 106,
    125, 127; philanthropic discounting
    in, 23, 118–24; projected evolution
    of problems in, 107–12; value expres-
    sion of donors in, 116–18
Tisch, James, 14
top-down solutions, 22
transaction costs, 131–33
transparency, 8–9
Turner, Ted, 83–84

UN Foundation, 83–84
United Jewish Appeal-Federation of
    Jewish Philanthropies of New York
    City (UJA-Federation), 14
United Way, 130, 147–48
U.S. government bonds, 120

value parameters, ix, 4–5, 20–22, 167–
    71; balance of public and private
    dimensions in, 28–32, 39, 168–71;
    case studies of, 10–19; of charitable
    giving, 33–37; definition of, 160–61;
    of expressive giving, 32–34, 41–45,
    162–63; four forms of, 32–34, 142;
    of instrumental giving, 32–34, 37–
    40, 170–71; of payout rates, 116–18;
    of strategic giving, 45–50
vehicles for giving. See institutional forms
venture philanthropy, 91–99, 101, 150;
    consultative roles in, 95–96, 98–99;
    due diligence in, 93–94; engagement
    levels in, 96–98; for-profit aspects
    of, 94; performance measurement

in, 91, 94–95; personal satisfaction
in, 96–97
Virtual Foundation, 149–50
virtual (Internet) foundations, 149–50

watchdog groups, 8
what to support. *See* value parameters

Wildlife Conservation Society (WCS),
10–14
Windham Foundation, 47–49
Wirth, Timothy, 84
W.K. Kellogg Foundation, 92
Women with Inherited Wealth initia-
tive, 151